GOOD ADVICE FROM

PROFESSIONAL WRESTLING

Full Contact Life Lessons

How to Get Over — and Stay There

by **Darren Paltrowitz** and **D.X. Ferris**

FOREWORD BY

Diamond Dallas Page

6623 **PRESS**

ANNOUNCERS' TABLE OF CONTENTS

Part I:
On Aspiration and Success

Part II:
On Wrestling

Locker Room

The Paltrocast with Darren Paltrowitz is a bi-weekly podcast produced by PureGrainAudio.com.

The Paltrocast features exclusive 20-minute-or-less interviews with top entertainers, entrepreneurs and other influencers.

We talk music, movies, productivity and more.

Prior guests include Chris Jericho, Diamond Dallas Page, Sophia Bush, Andrew W.K., Ace Frehley, Dennis Quaid, Dee Snider, Marc Summers, and *Games Of Thrones* star Hafthor Björnsson.

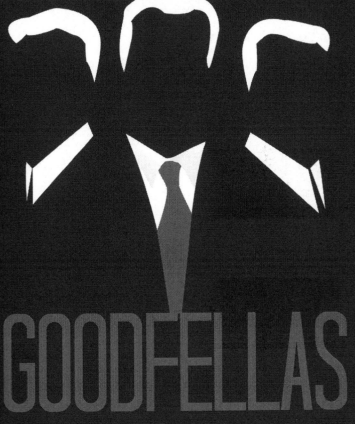

Write down some goals.

Checklists are the best way to make sure you do what you want & need to do.

You're allowed to write in (your own) books.

Don't trust anybody who tells you otherwise.

Where would you like to be in a year?

What can you do to move closer today?

METHODOLOGY & STYLE

On the following pages, some wrestlers are referred to by their stage names; some by their more conventional name. But sometimes their stage name is their legal name, which is a whole 'nother issue. Some wrestlers are touchy about seeing their real name in print, and they turn the issue into a *respect* thing. Regardless, you know who we're talking about. Don't be dense.

Metrics and statistics in wrestling are infamously unreliable. Belts famously change hands briefly. Some championship runs make it into the record books. Some don't. The WWE Universe now includes the whole ball of wax that used to be WWF, WCW (which was NWA but is not), and ECW. WWE has official counts, and we generally defer to those numbers. Maybe Ric Flair was a world champion 21, 16, or 25 times. You get the idea.

In periods discussed on the following pages, the organization we know as the WWE was the WWWF and the WWF. The WWE has its own policies about how to refer to it as what and when. That's their business. You know what we're talking about. Don't be a pencil neck.

Simlarly: Over the years, the WWE's Monday night wrestling program has been formally titled *Monday Night Raw*, *Raw is War*, and *WWE Raw*. The various belts' titles also morph over time. You see what we're saying.

All text and citations follow APE Style, with occasional deferral to the WWE's house style.

If you have a correction, you're probably right. To submit your comment, write it on a piece of paper, put it in a bottle, put a cork in it, shine it up real nice, turn it sideways, and...

Foreword: Forward

by Diamond Dallas Page

I didn't start wrestling until I was 35 years old. When I told Michael "P.S." Hayes — the wrestling legend, one of the Fabulous Freebirds — about my plans to get in the ring, he literally fell out of his chair laughing. Pretty much no one thought that Diamond Dallas Page would have a career as a pro wrestler... well, except Diamond Dallas Page.

I talk a lot about my journey as a wrestler in my book, *Positively Unstoppable: The Art Of Owning It*. But I have had a lot of different identities within my life. I've been a 12-year-old piece of near-roadkill on the Jersey Shore. A 29-year-old rock-and-dance club owner in Fort Myers. A 35-year-old rookie wrestler in Atlanta. A 43-year-old World Heavyweight Champion in Tacoma, the oldest ever to take that title. And I've been a 60-year-old WWE Hall of Famer in Orlando. Lots of overachieving in those last couple sentences, I'll admit.

Yet here's one of the major differences between DDP and most people dealing with challenges, setbacks and obstacles: I not only talk the talk. I walk the talk. I set a goal, I visualize the endgame. And I work as hard as I possibly can to make that goal a reality. It is not just in DDP Yoga that inspiration meets perspiration.

While I may not be giving Diamond Cutters in the ring 200+ days a year anymore, I still identify as a professional wrestler. Not only because my success in the wrestling business provided the launching pad for DDP Yoga. Not only is it because a lot of my best friends are — or were — professional wrestlers. It is also because it takes a lot of skills to make it in the world of wrestling.

As Darren and D.X. point out in this book, a professional wrestler is an athlete who can also act, perform and improvise in front of a live crowd. And the wrestler also has to look great while doing all of that. The business, like life, is always changing: Maybe you can't do what you used to. Maybe what you used to do doesn't work any more. Will you quit? Or will you adapt?

Like you, I had my chances to quit. I didn't. I adapted. I still am. These days, I am still on the road as much as I was in my wrestling heyday—fortunately, most of that alongside my beautiful wife and manager, Brenda—if not more. Wrestling prepared me for change. Wrestling teaches you how to meet challenges head-on. Wrestling has a lot to offer, even if you watch at home. That's where I started too.

I am proud of how far the wrestling business has come in recent years. So many of my brothers and sisters have also found success outside of the ring as business owners and performers in other industries. They have helped eliminate so many of the stigmas that were associated with professional wrestling from way back when. These days, wrestling is full of awesome people, and it's wonderful to see so many places for a wrestler to practice their craft.

With all of that said, by all means should you look to professional wrestling for some good advice. No matter where you are in life, it pays to study greatness. This book features insights from some of the true greats of the wrestling business. But no matter what you choose to do with that advice, be sure to own it — and feel the BANG!

Dallas Page

Wrestling Is Real

by Darren Paltrowitz

There is nothing quite like professional wrestling. It's a true mixture of sports and theatre, with roots that go back more than a century, to the world of carnival sideshows. But the entertainment-heavy form of wrestling we see today — which arguably began with Gorgeous George in the 1940s — is both mainstream and a billion-dollar industry.

While wrestling has seen economic peaks and valleys, it has never been as relevant as it is today. The president of the United States Of America was involved with several WrestleManias, including the main event in WrestleMania 23. WrestleMania — now an annual event for over 35 years — is essentially the Super Bowl of wrestling. Before the launch of the WWE's own subscription network, top pay-per-views sold over a million buys. Now WrestleMania's WWE Network viewers routinely rank in the millions. The stadium-sized live event routinely draws nearly 80,000 spectators.

WWE — World Wrestling Entertainment, Inc., the company behind WrestleMania — is not only a publicly traded company, but its stock is currently trading at a higher per-share price than General Electric, Ford, eBay and Bank Of America combined. The WWE Network has over 2 million subscribers. WWE's new five-year TV deals with Fox and NBCUniversal are together worth $2 billion, twice as much as the WWE was earning under its current contract.[1]

All the while, the company continues to own and develop intellectual property surrounding most of wrestling's greats, past and present, leaving the door open to successful merchandising opportunities for decades to come.

But as of early 2019, WWE's activity is far from the sum total of the entire wrestling business. In 2001, it looked like WWE was the only game in town. WWE CEO Vince McMahon and company acquired its two largest North American competitors: the Ted Turner-connected World Championship Wrestling, and Paul Heyman's Extreme Championship Wrestling. After all, since the 1980s, the company that became WWE had united wrestling from a continuum of competing regional territories into a national business. And it had also overcome many nationally minded competitors beyond WCW and ECW, vanquishing all comers, including the AWA, UWF, GWF, XWF, WWA...

No matter what high-powered investor, television partner or attached star power got involved, the WWE had not had viable competition since dissolving the WCW and ECW. Until the phenomenal 2018 show that was All In. Comprised of wrestlers from a variety of companies around the world — including the NWA, Ring of Honor, Impact Wrestling, New Japan Pro-Wrestling, and Mexico's CMLL and AAA — the international all-star show sold out the Sears Centre outside Chicago, Illinois, in about 30 minutes after tickets went on sale.

The one-off live event holds the distinction of being the first non-WWE or WCW-promoted wrestling event in the United States to sell over 10,000 tickets in well over 20 years. And that sellout occurred before fans even knew who would headline in the main event.

That same weekend as All In, wrestling podcast champion Conrad Thompson presented Starrcast, a four-day professional wrestling fan convention. With participation from over 120 wrestlers, wrestling personalities and podcasters, the event included WWE Hall of Famers and current independent stars alike. Attendance at the Hyatt Regency Chicago reportedly topped 10,000. Plans for another Starrcast followed.

The success of the All In show—which intentionally overlapped with Starrcast — led to the long-rumored announcement of a new wrestling company, All Elite Wrestling. Bankrolled by the same billionaire Khan family that owns the NFL's Jacksonville Jaguars, AEW is led by the trio of wrestlers who masterminded All In: Cody Rhodes and the phenom tag team The Young Bucks, plus notables like Kenny Omega. AEW scheduled its debut pay-per-view in May 2019, at the MGM Arena in Las Vegas, with an imminent TV deal all but inevitable.

One month prior to the success of the historical All In event, the Ring of Honor and New Japan Pro-Wrestling promotions had already announced a show at New York's Madison Square Garden April 6, 2019 — during the WWE's WrestleMania Weekend, for those keeping score. As with All In, fans did not know of the main-event or most of the card's participating talent when the show went on-sale in August 2018. Yet within minutes, the ROH/NJPW G1 Supercard sold out all available tickets.

And as the saying goes, good things come in threes. In 2018, Chris Jericho's Rock 'N' Wrestling Rager at Sea was a four-night cruise co-produced with Sixthman — a company which has helmed celebrity-oriented cruises for the likes of Kiss, Jon Bon Jovi, Kid Rock, *Impractical Jokers* and *The Walking Dead* — and co-hosted by wrestling legend Jericho. The Rager at Sea brought together Jericho's long-held interests in wrestling, music, comedy, podcasts and fitness, including talent from multiple wrestling promotions, like All In and ROH/ NJPW G1 Supercard did. Not surprisingly, this independently produced, internationally minded, sold-out wrestling event also drew thousands of fans. And the all-inclusive nature of the cruise — which will be returning for a second edition — seemed to position Jericho to claim a starring role in the AEW ranks.

Beyond those wrestling companies and events, many other wrestling companies are making people around the world take notice. MLW airs weekly on beIN SPORTS. The Mexican-centric Lucha Underground is available through Netflix and the El Rey Network. Dojo Pro streams through Amazon Prime. England's WhatCulture Pro Wrestling — WCPW, for short — stages notable internet pay-per-views. Scotland's Insane Championship Wrestling has been rumored to be in discussions with WWE about possible collaborations, while Progress Wrestling is already working with WWE. Simply put, this is a great time to be a wrestling fan. There is no shortage of great wrestling content to watch every week.

The wrestling business itself continues to be full of popping, talented performers whose behind-the-scene actions may be more interesting than their in-ring performances. On the current WWE roster, Xavier Woods has a Ph.D. in educational psychology.

David Otunga is a graduate of Harvard Law School. Chad Gable was a U.S. Olympic wrestler. Chris Jericho not only still draws big crowds as a wrestler, but he is also the host of a popular podcast (*Talk Is Jericho*), the singer of a popular band (Fozzy) and the author of four published memoirs. WWE Hall of Famer Jim Ross has a line of barbecue sauces. WWE Hall of Famer Diamond Dallas Page invented a globally renowned fitness program called DDP Yoga. Former WWE Heavyweight Champion "JBL" John Bradshaw Layfield is a commentator for Fox News. Dwayne "The Rock" Johnson is arguably the world's top movie star. The days of wrestlers simply being rejects from football and bodybuilding are inarguably a thing of the past.

Consider what it takes to be a professional wrestler. As in any art, the odds are stacked against any aspiring individual, no matter how gifted. The majority of them not only have to be physically capable of doing stunts, but also good enough actors to sell their characters, to make crowds believe in them, and root for them —or against them. Wrestlers come from all backgrounds, in all shapes and sizes. Yet all of them must have enough dramatic presence and street smarts to survive life on the road. This path of a pro wrestler entails working well with others and altogether knowing how to go with the flow, to ensure that each grappler is doing their best to please bosses, peers and audiences alike — perhaps while portraying an in-ring persona that may have little in common with their true self. In turn, wrestlers tend to have a lot in common with artists like musicians and comedians — more so than traditional competitive athletes.

We all want to be better at something. But no matter what that goal is, getting where you want to be means you'll have to climb over — or fight through — many of the same obstacles. We're all building with the same blocks, using the same tools. A positive mental attitude is key: P.M.A. is the best fuel. And it's free. You need to know what you are pursuing. You need to believe you can make things happen. Persistence is also important; you are unlikely to accomplish your goals if you give up easily. And unexpectedly, when you have arrived where you wanted to be, you will undoubtedly begin to look further ahead, hoping for more success.

Given the exceptional odds you need to overcome to succeed in the world of professional wrestling — and outside it, too — why not look to wrestlers, managers and promoters for some sage advice? Ferris and I have compiled some inspirational notes and quotes from some of wrestling's most successful, notable and notorious individuals. Read through the following pages and think about how their exciting careers apply to your everyday existence, no matter your job or lifestyle. Expect to laugh and learn —and when you put down the book, you can go back to your day, energized and excited.

Professional Wrestling

by D.X. Ferris

Professional wrestling is America. You don't have to like wrestling. You don't have to respect it. But if you don't understand it, you will lose. If you *do* study it and learn from it, it can teach you to win.

Professional wrestling is the pinnacle of human performance. It's an athletic discipline. *And* it's the ultimate application of the liberal arts. It's a distinct hybrid form of competition and cooperation. It's show business turned up to 11. Pro wrestlers don't fight to win. To get over—read: "earn undeniable appreciation"—a wrestler needs to *radiate* excellence, from their traps to their improvised comments.

In some ways, wrestling is like other entertainment: It can be an amusing distraction that you never think about again after this week's three-hour *Raw* is over. Or you can watch closely, pay attention, take some notes, and do some outside reading about it. And if you do, all that TV time becomes an investment, a weekly meditation, a ongoing case study in what it takes to make it. Even if you wear a skirt or tie all day, and you'll never take a single bump.

You spend a lot of time and money following wrestling. You should *get* something from it. And make no mistake: The much-maligned field is, in fact, not only inspiring, but educational. It's far from fake. It's *really* demanding.

Your favorite wrestlers put their body on the line. They live in pain so you can have someone to cheer... or maybe boo. They do that for you. And this brutal, beautiful spectacle is good for so much more than brief pops and fading chants.

Granted, pro wrestling isn't for everybody. Not everybody deserves it. Some people look down on wrestling. They don't like awesome things that are fun. That's their problem. The art is a rich tradition filled with punishing challenges. To paraphrase a famous chairman of a board: If you can make it there, you can make it anywhere

Not for nothing is it called *professional* wrestling.

To be a next-level success in professional wrestling, you need the same foundation of basic skills that will make you successful in any other business. **Most successful wrestlers can...**

1) Speak well. Especially in public. If you cannot speak effectively, you probably have a limited future.

2) Write well. A star wrestler can cut a good promo — that is, say some colorful and catchy things about their worthy opponents and hated rivals. If you can't use words to generate additional interest in your work, you have limited potential.

3) Look the part. For most of us, cultivating the right look is as simple as buying a good-looking business outfit. But most wrestlers need to physically transform their body into their business card, over the course of millions of reps and sprints. And then they still need to tie it all together, from their hair to their boots. If you don't look the part, most people will overlook your potential.

4) Use computers. In the 21st century, being good at the work isn't enough to make a wrestler successful. A fan-favorite needs to connect with his audience in person, over TV, and — day in, day out — online, via social media. If you can't use technology, you'll wind up working harder and earning less, whether you're a nurse, writer, mechanic, or jobber.

5) Talk the talk. Every profession has a specialized vocabulary, words that workers use to discuss phemomena, trends, and routine interactions. True pros don't just show up and do whatever.

They execute a detailed plan, which they assemble using an arsenal of clearly defined terms. From a job interview to a sales call, you need to prove you know what you are talking about.

Wrestlers need to do all the things that will make someone successful as a corporate human resources executive, fireman, or ballerina. And so many more aptitudes, habits, and attitudes of highly effective people can help you cultivate success in the squared circle or out, from cubicle culture to sports.

Successful professional wrestlers not only display all those foundational core competencies — but they do it all while taking a beating.

Even though a wrestling match is not a true fight, it is always a demanding physical display. Wrestlers live with pain and uncertainty, in a business that makes demands like few others. Wrestling, after all, is a business that has *multiple* terms to describe the practice of literally cutting yourself open and bleeding to enhance your presentation.

Imagine delivering a passionate PowerPoint presentation... then running around the office for 20 minutes, leaping off a desk, and crashing through a conference table. And *then* rising, only to be whacked in the head with a folding chair. And looking good while you do it. That's what wrestlers do. It's true.

Look at the picture of Salina de la Renta on page 71. Does she look like she's headed to a *Playboy* photo shoot? She would definitely be welcomed at one — but she's dressed for success, like she's headed to a board room. In the 21st century, *that* is what a wrestling MVP looks like.

And that, fellow fans, is the life of a professional wrestler. Success in this squared circle requires business savvy. It involves a cut-throat sense of interpersonal politics. The best in the biz have a canny grasp of human psychology. Even the lowliest dark-match major-leaguers possess superhuman cardiovascular fitness.

It's a uniquely demanding art. Ballerinas and acrobats practice similar physical discipline. But none of them fly from a turnbuckle and drop onto a hard mat, with nothing to cushion their fall except some hard-won technique.

And try to think of a more consequential application of the liberal arts. What could be a bigger responsibility than *talking* 20,000 people into the local arena, by creating a dramatic scenario that throngs of believers *need* to witness? Pro wrestling's weaponized strain of rhetoric, while distinct, is not unique.

WWE Hall of Fame inductee — Class of 2013 — Donald J. Trump literally talked his way into the White House, using a pro-wrestling mode of public speech. President Trump zings his opponents. He annihilates them with unshakeable nicknames. He rejects all formal argumentation and presents himself as the biggest, meanest badass in the building. He sold the USA on his version of an American dream promo. And he has been unstoppable. Democrat and Republican, the entire field of career speechmakers are helpless before the hard-charging fast talker who cut his teeth in WWE pay per views.

Professional wrestling has changed American culture and shaped the entire world. It can mold your life for the better. So get ready to learn useful lessons from some of the best who ever did it.

"I can go further because of what I just saw."

— Patton Oswalt

"People tend to write off athletic pursuits as being entirely physical, and they're not. I think this is an easy way for people to look at it that don't engage, or that never thought about playing anything at a very high level. [It] requires some intense thinking... understanding what's required, understanding when and how to exectue, understanding how to keep your sh*t together under pressure — those are all intensely intellectual aspects of any really high-end athletic pursuit."

— Joe Rogan

"If I don't keep going at this, nothing is going to happen."

— Steve Basilone

This book is brought to you by

Seven Day Grind

Get Home and Work More

Wake Up So Early It Hurts

Pay Now Play Later

Cold Showers

and

D.I.Y.M.F.S.

#DoTheWork

Part I:

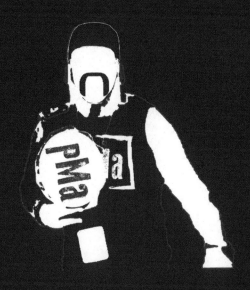

Pro Wrestling Greats on Career Aspirations and Success

Ric Flair was an active in-ring performer for over 30 years. He's widely regarded as the greatest professional wrestler of all time. Flair created a timeless character in the brash, polished, immaculately dressed, unwaveringly confident "The Nature Boy"… with some inspiration from Buddy Rogers, an earlier all-time great who achieved fame before Flair using the same moniker. In some capacity, Flair worked with virtually every notable main-event talent of the 1970s, 1980s, 1990s and 2000s. His in-ring work still holds up all these years later.

Flair started using his trademark catch phrase "To be the man, you've got to beat the man" in the 1980s. At the time, he was not yet the stylin', profilin', limousine-ridin', global icon he would become. But he was on the way, chest-chopping and *woo*ing all comers.

The best and *the biggest* are singular distinctions. There can only be one. Flair's catch phrase was a challenge and promise: He would be *the* one. If you want to be the one, you need to defeat the recognized person at the top of the game.

Granted, every wrestling company had its own version of "The Man," a grappler who is recognized as the world champion… in the local region. In the

21st century, "the man" doesn't even need to be a man. When you wear a world-championship belt, there is little doubt who the man is. WWE Women's Champion Becky Lynch took the belt *and* the title, declaring herself The Man, making the coveted distinction gender-neutral. (In March 2019, Lynch was announced as one of the first women to headline a WrestleMania.)

You don't have to be a wrestler to be The Man. No matter your profession or hobby, that title applies to anyone who undoubtedly leads, excels, sets the standard, or altogether matters. If you are the public face of an organization, then you are The Man.

(If you want to be The Woman or The One, go for it — when you create something undeniable, you can make your own rules.)

In the case of Ric Flair, sometimes being The Man meant looking cool while other people were doing the heavy lifting. Sometimes he made himself look worse to create a better match and put over his fellow wrestlers. Once in character, he wasn't afraid to look hurt or scared. In any given match, he did what was right for the business. There is not just one way to become The Man. It's hard to gain recognition as The Man if you're chasing your own glory and you're not truly leading a winning team.

So whatever you choose to do, ask yourself:

Are you are the one everybody looks to?

If you are not, what is getting in the way of that happening?

Who is in the way?

Is it you?

Are you the problem?

Or are you The Man?

> **"Headlining WrestleMania is making it... We always want more, and we're always looking to climb up the ladder."**
>
> **— Big E**

Before Big E joined the WWE, he was a high school state champion wrestler in Florida, then a collegiate football player, and a USA Powerlifting champion. Within WWE's NXT development system, Big E — then using the moniker "Big E Langston" — was a dominant competitor. He would set the bar higher for himself, insisting on pinning his competitors with a five-count. (If you're keeping score at home, that's two more than the traditional three-count for a victory.)

As of this writing, the WWE is not only the largest wrestling-related company, but also where the majority of wrestlers want to be working. WWE programming is broadcast in more countries than any other wrestling promotion's sports entertainment, as WWE calls its form of competition.

With a cast of dozens and different troupes, the company presents more live events than most touring acts. Its merchandising operation provides some of the entertainment industry's rare indisputable metrics. In 2018, the company reported its highest quarterly earnings in its history, $281.6 million.[2] Headlining a WrestleMania truly means a wrestler is at the top of their field, in the big ring at the big show.

Big E is in it to win it. Emphasizing the competitive nature of WWE, he wants to be at the top of the top, not in the middle of the pack. He's not content to merely have a spot in the show. He wants to be an undisputed achiever, a top performer. He expects top performers to perform. Once he reached the big leagues, he didn't relax and coast. He saw an opportunity for more work. You work harder than you ever have to make it to the top. And then you work harder if you want to stay there.

"Deserve" is a tricky issue in work and life. People who want more dwell on what they (think) they deserve. People who deserve more are busy working more. How can you demonstrate what you truly deserve? People who do more tend to get more. Set your goals high. Look at the people around you. Set your goals higher.

Even if you helped put the company where it is… Even if you had a great yesterday… If you're not earning your keep today, why is your business keeping you around?

E's ambition applies to all industries and interests.

Aspire to be the best at what you do.

Don't phone it in.

If you do, someone who is more hungry than you is ready and willing to take your spot.

In competition, if you're lucky and the timing is right, maybe you'll get what you earned today — not yesterday.

What you *deserve*?

Don't tell your bosses. Show them.

> "My brother told me 'You don't want to be like your idols; you want to grow up and be better than them.'"

> — AJ Lee

AJ Lee was an against-all-odds story in the WWE. She was not the physical type the company preferred. Signed in the Divas era, she was considerably smaller than many of her peers. However, Lee worked her way up to the top of women's wrestling. In time, she became one of the few woman to play a part of major storylines with top male talent like John Cena, Daniel Bryan and Kane.

AJ Lee is also one of the few WWE athletes to leave the company on her own terms, while still working at the top. She has since found success as an author. Her book *Crazy is My Superpower: How I Triumphed by Breaking Bones, Breaking Hearts and Breaking The Rules* has been optioned for television development. And she has plenty of other non-wrestling projects in development. Lee has blazed her own path — or, more accurately, paths.

Lee has a healthy but competitive attitude toward her idols. She doesn't have time for hero worship. Her heroes' best achievements are an obstacle, not a finish line. The are inspiration, not a target. A starting point, not a template. She doesn't what to do what some people have done before. She wants to exceed it. She wants to do her own thing.

Lee's quote applies to your personal and professional endeavors. Just because someone accomplished something major, it does not mean that you cannot surpass or improve upon their accomplishment.

Think of what your idols have done as a suggestion rather than mandatory to-do list. You have the potential to be someone's role model.

Will you lead or follow?

Inspire or imitate?

> **"Your destiny is what you make. It's the choices that you make. And for every choice, there's a consequence."**
>
> **— Triple H**

Triple H is in rare company, accomplished inside the ring and out. His achievements are big and broad, whether he's pushing paper or wielding a sledgehammer.

When it comes to storyline-based accolades, few performers have held as many titles or worked in as many main events.

As a hands-on executive, his latest title in the multi-billion dollar company is Executive Vice President of Talent, Live Events and Creative.

Backstage, Triple H has mentored the new generation WWE stars, as the current executive overseeing the developmental branch NXT.

Amazingly, Triple H is still active as an in-ring competitor and on-screen performer, the most visible active veteran of the Attitude Era. He also makes media appearances on behalf of the WWE, which few of the company's executives do. Very few people would have predicted that the WCW wrestler formerly known as Terra Ryzin would still working at the top over 20 years after debuting in the WWF as Hunter Hearst Helmsley.

Renowned for his political acumen, Triple H has worked his way into his unique spot and made himself a pivotal figure in the history of professional wrestling.

Most people think of destiny in a mystical sense of the term, a predetermined surprise that is ultimately out of their control— hopefully a pleasant one.

But when the hard-nosed Triple H talks about destiny, he is referring the very calculable cumulative results from an ongoing series of choices, actions, effort and momentum. To Triple H, a destination is not a mystery; you arrive where you go. It's mathematics, not magic.

As the saying goes, you are what you eat. It's applicable to every facet of your life. Input affects output.

You are the sum of the people you know, the things you do, and the experiences you have.

Keep in mind the choices you make and the path you chart. They will determine your destination.

"Life is 10 percent what happens to you and 90 percent how you react to it."

— Diamond Dallas Page

Wrestling is only one of the areas which DDP has succeeded. Beyond writing, acting and motivational speaking, DDP is the founder of DDP Yoga. An internationally renowned fitness system like no other, DDPY is where, as DDP's mantra goes, "inspiration meets perspiration."

DDP has long preached — and practiced — basic concepts like persistence, positivity and believing in yourself. When talks about "living life at 90 percent," he reminds you to focus on your reactions, more so than what has happened to you. According to DDP, what is happening now is of the utmost importance — not what has happened to you at any point in the past.

No matter your career path, family background or the social situation at hand, living life at 90 percent applies to you. Prioritizing the present is what's important. It keeps you on your path, focused on who, what, where, why and how things are going around you. If you think of every situation as a new development and a different opportunity, you have a better chance to avoid making the same mistakes you made in the past.

You may have strong feelings about the past — maybe anger or resentment.

Everybody does.

But if you dwell on them, you are wasting today's energy on something you cannot change. Don't let the past drain limited resources like time and energy. If you have to think about the past, let it fuel your motion forward.

If your past contains something good, think about how you create another situation like the good time.

If your past still lingers and provides fresh pain, think about what you can do to move away from it.

Move forward.

As NFL coaching legend Vince Lombardi said, "The spirit, the will to win, and the will to excel are the things that endure. These qualities are so much more important than the events that occur."[3]

"The best chance you have if you wanna rise to top is to give yourself loneliness, fear nothing and work hard. One thing you will discover: Life is the best lesson... You have learned much more than you think. And what you have inside was there right from the beginning."

— Bret Hart

When actual *wrestling* was a more important part of the business, Bret "The Hitman" Hart billed himself as "The Best There Is, the Best There Was, and the Best There Ever Will Be." Few argued the point.

It's easy to understand why Hart was so highly regarded. He is a second generation wrestler, raised by one of the business' legendary true grapplers and tough guys, Stu Hart. His pedigree definitely helped; he grew up in a extended network of globe-touring wrestlers. But his career and success were firmly on his own shoulders. His own hard work made him successful.

Hart didn't just wrestle well. He presented it well. His matches were always focused on storytelling. No matter the skill level of the other wrestlers, you knew a Bret Hart match would be special because he was involved.

In this quote, when Hart talks about loneliness, he is not emphasizing being a loner or intentionally antisocial. You need time and space to learn your true self. Give yourself permission. And understand it has a cost. To succeed in any field, you need to miss social opportunities to develop yourself and your craft.

What are you willing to miss to make your goals a reality?

Work hard. Keep moving forward. Don't let fear stop you.

Learn to recognize fear.

Stare it down.

Move past it.

It pays to be great at what you do. Greatness stems from practice and repetition.

Often, the people around you won't understand what you are trying to build. Don't wait for their approval. Don't wait them to recognize your excellence, value, or potential.

Develop yourself.

Success depends on what you do today. Then doing the right things on a long-term basis.

Commit to a consistent focus.

You can't let dreams get in the way of reality. The dreams of youths are nothing more than the regrets of tomorrow."

— Larry Zbyszko

Larry Zbyszko had a longer career than many people may realize. The WWE Hall of Famer was a main-eventer in the early 1980s, battling Bruno Sammartino in a longrunning feud. His later WCW run included time as a broadcaster, which tied into a major storyline alongside Scott Hall and the NWO.

Dreams are useful when they function as goals.

Dreams can be harmful when they function as expectations.

Dreams change. One person's fantasy can be another person's nightmare. Your dreams as a teenager may have little to do with your dreams as an adult. After all, money, family, health and other personalized factors are likely to influence what you want to accomplish.

Dreams may keep you going through hard times.

But if you don't put in the work to make those dreams reality, yesterday's dreams can become the waking nightmare that is regret.

Only you know what your dreams are. Only you can pursue those dreams.

If you don't work to achieve your dreams, you have surrendered to a reality of somebody else's making.

If you are not pursuing your dreams, you are building tomorrow's regrets.

Regrets will never add any fun — nor any value — to your life.

"Success isn't always about greatness. It's about consistency."

— The Rock

As of this writing, Dwayne Johnson is one of the biggest movie stars in the world, if not the biggest. He's an a A-list actor with a following in motion pictures, television, and live events. He achieved fame in the wrestling world, as the exuberant character known as The Rock, in the WWE's Attitude Era, when every Monday night *Raw* felt like a movie. He also remains popular and present in wrestling, still making the occasional WWE appearance. All the while, Johnson is still a family man, stays in tip-top shape, maintains a flawless reputation, employs thousands of people, and generates a lot of income.

Movie metrics site The Numbers ranked Johnson as its no. 1 box-office star for 2018, based on a three-year domestic gross of $983 million dollars.[4] (*Forbes* ranked him no. 10 for the year, but we are talking about consistency.[5]) According to *Business Insider*, he is already the no. 20 all-time top-grossing movie star, with a lifetime take of over $3 billion.[6]

Johnson leads by example. He is already the focus of several entire motivational books. He accomplishes so much on a regular basis that he's a real-life superhero, a true Hercules, a legend in his own time.

Johnson's secret to success is very straightforward: Emphasize consistency.

To stay in great shape physically, you need to consistently follow a diet and exercise regimen.

To stay gainfully employed, you need to consistently show up for work — and be someone who others want to work with.

Greatness is not a one-off happenstance.

Look at all of your current projects and dealings. Ask yourself: Are you are being consistent?

If you are not, what is keeping you from consistency?

Even consistent small actions can move mountains.

Maybe you don't have the time or energy to executive-produce a Hollywood franchise or work out at four in the morning.

You don't have to do everything The Rock does.

You can do some of it.

If you only put five or ten minutes of work towards your ideal goal, 365 days of consistent work will add up.

Do some pushups. After dinner, ride an exercise bike while you watch a sitcom rerun.

Write a page a day. Start working on a book, a script, a song, or something else productive — something you can't do now, but you might be able to do in time.

Develop a superpower of your own.

"Hard work pays off.
Dreams come true. Bad
times don't last, but bad
guys do."

— Scott Hall

Scott Hall is a contender for wrestling's Mount Rushmore. After runs in WCW, the AWA and Japan, he made it to the WWF in the early 1990s, as Razor Ramon. Once he was at the big show, Hall quickly established himself as a top draw, finding success as both a heel (the kind of colorful bad guy the crowds love to hate) and a babyface (a traditional good guy).

This success was miniscule compared to what he accomplished as one of the lead members of the WCW's New World Order clique, one of the greatest stories in the history of the sport. His NWO stardom kept him going through further runs in WWE and TNA.

Sadly, Hall almost became a premature wrestling casualty. Wear, tear and physical pain from life in the ring led to substance abuse issues. Numerous attempts at rehab failed, even though the WWE and many wrestling peers directly tried to help him.

As chronicled in the documentary *The Resurrection of Jake the Snake*, Hall was barely functional, and had given up hope until Diamond Dallas Page came to the rescue. Hall is now healthy, doing well, living clean, and greeting fans at conventions all over the country.

People remember what you do, the good and the bad. If you manage to make an impression, once you commit to a positive path, they will root for you — as Hall said in his WWE Hall of Fame induction speech. While he has been widely known as "the bad guy" for more of his career than not, Hall remains popular and universally respected. In his case, his enduring legacy as a heel means he is remembered as someone who defied authority, took risks, and rebelled against the business' status quo.

The takeaways from Hall's philosophy:

Bad times are not permanent. Hard work will help you prevail.

You can get yourself out of a rut.

You can work yourself out of a corner.

You can make positive changes to your situation.

Ultimately, you can help create something that people will remember favorably, long into the future.

So do something memorable.

> "Although timing in life is everything, memorable moments in history don't just happen! Do something…. Stay positive!"
>
> — Lita

Lita broke many a barrier as a WWF performer, flying over some of them. When she joined the company, her look and wardrobe immediately separated her from the other wrestlers —women and men. She became her own island of cool culture. She also came across as a true fan of wrestling. In one impressive, high-flying move after another, she displayed athleticism rarely seen from many of the female wrestlers that had come before her.

In the mid-2000s, Lita announced her in-ring retirement due to nagging injuries. She announced a new goal, and she pursued a career in music. As a musician, she found a new worldwide audience, and she toured internationally. She slowly found her way back into the wrestling world as a trainer and announcer. Fans were shocked when Lita announced an in-ring comeback in 2018, as a marquee draw for WWE's Evolution event.

In this quote, Lita notes the common maxim, "Timing is everything."

She also points that true accomplishments do not simply happen. To make history, people need to take action.

And she repeats the phrase that has been a foundation of the self-improvement field for almost a century, since Napoleon Hill's seminal book *Think and Grow Rich*: Cultivate a positive attitude.

Lita's ups and downs are applicable to your career, no matter your field.

Waiting for the phone to ring rarely yields results. Doing something great will make that phone ring. Scouts and recruiters are generally looking for people who already have something going on. The people who can hire you want accomplishments, not potential.

Approaching your work with a negative disposition is also unlikely to bring you closer toward where you want to be. Sometimes, as Lita notes, you are at the mercy of timing.

Maybe you weren't in the right place at the right time — the previous time, in the past. But if you are always ready, prepared, and able to put the work in, your odds of succeeding are better when that ideal opportunity does present itself.

Even in the bad times, even in slow periods, work on yourself.

Try to make something good happen.

And be ready when it does.

"Everybody on top has a ton of haters."

— Diamond Dallas Page

As wrestling's king of P.M.A., Diamond Dallas Page has shared enough positivity-oriented quotes to fill a book — or, more precisely, two books... in addition to a popular, life-changing franchise of home videos and online tutorials, from workouts to nuritional guides. If motivational quotes are gems, the master of The Diamond Cutter has the world's most productive mine.

Smart positive people will acknowledge negatives.

To defeat a negative situation, you need to acknowledge it.

Too often, the mantra "keep it positive" ignores the negative and meaningful realities of a situation.

Some people make negativity their business. Instead of pursuing their own goals, the position themselves as a professional judge of others. They become haters who idly spend time and energy expressing disdain, not appreciation, for others involved in productive activity. A hater can find the negativity in any situation.

But a positive person can find something good in any situation. Look closely, and you'll always leave with a positive takeaway.

No one can rise to the top of any field without earning the resentment of others.

Jealousy and complaining are natural instincts.

We don't have to act on every negative impulse. And we can ignore them. But ignoring them takes some practice. We need to wrestle with our negative instincts.

Envy and jealousy bubble up in people who wish they had accomplished a particular feat themselves.

Most commentary comes from people who aren't on the field, or even in the game. After all, how many music critics themselves have written a hit song or headlined an arena? How many columnists could officiate an NFL game, throw a touchdown, or make it through a single day of training camp? How many years of training does a hater need to open an Instagram account and comment on a wrestler's posts?

People don't need certification or any sort of license to publicly criticize a hard-working woman or man. So hate can come at you at any time, from any number of directions. Often, it comes from people who aren't busy, who have time on their hands. Haters chose not to spend their days developing their own projects or skills. They don't want to work on themselves. They want to talk about you.

Don't let someone else's negativity interfere as you do what you do.

Remind yourself to consider the source. Maybe there is some truth in some of that criticism. And maybe some of it can be applied in a way that helps you improve your craft.

But sometimes haters just want to hate. It's what they do.

They made their choice.

Now make yours.

"It doesn't matter if people love you or hate you, as long as they feel strongly one way or the other. The worst place you can be is in the middle."

— Eric Bischoff

Eric Bischoff was one of the few talents who had successful tenures with the WWE, WCW, TNA and AWA. Bischoff is also a successful producer on a variety of non-wrestling projects, including television shows and video games. He is a popular podcaster, hosting the weekly *83 Weeks With Eric Bischoff* podcast alongside Conrad Thompson.

Bischoff was the public face of the WCW's historic high-water mark, when the company successfully went toe-to-toe with WWF, from the mid-90s through 2001.

During his wrestling heyday, Bischoff stood out from the pack by simultaneously taking on a variety of roles, on-screen and off. During his WCW run, he not only handled talent relations and produced the actual television programming being watched by millions. He also served as an on-camera performer, occasionally getting in the ring. After working for the WWE as an on-screen general manager, Bischoff broke down the business in the New York *Times* best-selling book *Controversy Creates Cash*, in which he opened up about his whole career.

This *Controversy Creates Cash* quote highlights Bischoff's goals, strategy, and strength as a communicator: He gets people to pay attention.

After decades as a cult product, wrestling became a mainstream fixture when it embraced storytelling, narratives, long-form tales people could follow and even participate in, as chanting members of the audience.

Worldwide, modest crowds would gather to watch wrestling matches in theaters and gyms and arenas. But when pro wrestling prioritized storylines over in-ring performances, international audiences tuned in to watch multiple sold-out arena shows, 52 weeks a year — and, for special occasion, sold-out stadium events.

Pro wrestling had always risen and fallen. But once people like Bischoff started telling exciting stories about colorful characters doing amazing, disruptive things, they grabbed the world's attention, and they kept it. We were hooked.

Through his career, Bischoff made seemingly impossible promises—and lived up to them.

He turned the languishing WCW from an unprofitable company to the top-rated wrestling company within a few years. He did it by creating original content that got people talking. WCW went supernova with the longrunning New World Order/NWO angle, in which a group of loudmouth heels threatened to destroy the very company fans were watching and everybody they tuned in to see. There was almost nothing positive, redeeming, or admirable about the NWO. Yet they were gripping. You couldn't wait to see what dirty deed they would stage next. Likable, they were not. Compelling, yes they were. They made the world react.

In your case, you probably do not want your audience to hate you, whether they're clients, readers, viewers, or co-workers.

But there are many better places to be than the middle.

Graphic design, human resources, popular music, network sitcoms — in every field, modern professionalism has been infected with a defining ethic of frictionless professionalism. Even people in creative fields are afraid to unleash a product that gets a reaction.

We are trained to make fearful, noncommittal choices because herd mentality tells us not to stand out. If you *want* to be a standout — especially a breakout star — in your field, you can't remain in the middle of the pack.

The people in the middle don't usually get awards or public recognition. Nor do they usually get the financial rewards when things are going well for a company.

You need to attract attention.

The best way to do it?

Practice excellence. Excel.

So take some risks . Make yourself memorable. It is a better alternative than being faceless and forgettable.

Don't be average.

Don't be in the middle.

Cody and Delirious. By Will Byington, courtesy Sixthman.

"I was cruising along in college, but I never lost sign of my wrestling aspirations. It was still all I wanted. So when a three-week tour of Winnipeg came up, I was going, school or not."

— Edge

Edge is a WWE Hall of Famer who had almost as many WWE title reigns — 31, according to the company —as anyone who ever worked for the McMahons, including 11 runs as the WWE champion and World Heavyweight champ. After countless main events, Edge was forced to retire from wrestling after a neck injury.

Beyond wrestling, Edge has become a successful actor. He has also continued to work with WWE, making occasional on-screen appearances, and also working with WWE Studios and the WWE Network. In recent years, he has been working outside the WWE universe, building a mainstream crossover success story as an actor.

When Edge talks about making hard choices, he is not just talking about wrestling. The key to success is being obsessed your industry of choice.

Think about the career path you are chosen.

What do you want?

What do you *really* want?

Are you willing to settle for something else, make a safe play, and accept a reasonable alternative?

What will you sacrifice for a chance at to do what you want to do?

Once you're headed toward your goal, here's the one sure way to *not* acheive it: Pursue a different goal. Follow a different path.

If you want to acheive you dreams, you might have to let go of something you want less.

And if you choose something you want less, because it's a safe bet... maybe you want that comfort and stability more than your dreams.

Do you have dreams, or do you have goals?

What do you want most?

Go get it.

"I've main-evented WrestleMania a handful of times, but it never gets old. It's the same with nerves."

— Randy Orton

Randy Orton was the youngest World Heavyweight Champion in WWE history, reaching that accolade at the age of 24. Highlights from his 20-year run include wearing the strap as a Triple Crown Champion and Grand Slam Champion. Orton is a third-generation competitor, and he has surpassed his father and grandfather in terms of popularity and mainstream recognition.

Still working in main events for the WWE, Randy Orton remains at the top of the card more than 15 years after debuting as part of the Evolution stable. Orton has headlined WrestleManias. He has also built up his IMDb credits substantially in recent years, appearing in both WWE and non-WWE-produced television and film projects.

All the while, Orton is also recognizable to even non-wrestling fans thanks to the "RKO Outta Nowhere" memes.

Orton says success never gets old. In the ring and out, change is constant. It takes more to succeed in a business where no two days are the same. Long-term growth is never routine.

Life at the top is exciting because he loves his job, and the stakes are high. Even after the better part of two decades, he doesn't take his success for granted. He still gets nervous before performing. Orton may seem cool and collected when in the midst of performing, but physically and emotionally, he is far from calm.

Sometimes that's a good thing.

Orton's sentiments apply to anyone who has to truly perform, whether it is in a high-profile sporting event or putting your name on a PowerPoint presentation. You need to stay hungry and live in the moment. Nervous energy and fear are two more natural instincts that are unavoidable if you work in a field that involves progress and risk — even when you are executing a task you have performed hundreds of times before.

Recognize your instincts. Lock up with them.

Embrace the opportunity for some spontaneous activity.

You've been there before. You know what to do.

And if you haven't been there before, practice until you recognize the feelings, the flows, the bumps and the rushes.

And that nervous energy you're worried about? Perhaps that's what makes you exciting to watch.

> ## "No WWE talent becomes a legend on their own."

> ## — The Ultimate Warrior

The Ultimate Warrior, who passed away suddenly in 2014, remains one of the most memorable characters in the WWE's storied history. Hulk Hogan passed him the torch at WrestleMania VI, and the Warrior was a champion during one of wrestling's peak eras. The Warrior was a singular figure and solitary presence. But he didn't achieve iconic status alone.

Most wrestlers approach the ring slowly, performing a dramatic entrance, letting excitement build in a slow simmer. The Warrior entered every match with a high-energy, hard-charging sprint, bursting from the back of the arena to its center. Few performers before or since the Warrior have created as much excitement as he did by merely entering the ring.

Charisma aside, The Ultimate Warrior was not one of wrestling's great in-ring performers. Wrestling rosters are famous for their sense of all-for-one brotherhood and bonded fraternity. In contrast, the Warrior was not known for being friendly with the majority of his wrestling cohorts. Instead, he opted to travel alone and keep to himself backstage. But after retiring from the ring, Warrior did work as a motivational speaker, keeping P.M.A. a focal point of his appearances.

Even though the Warrior's matches were never especially long — and also usually included minimal offense from his competitor(s) — he understood the importance of his opponent in any match. Like a waltz, wrestling generally involves two people whose movements work in tandem. Their cooperation tells a story through both athletic and artistic expression.

The best wrestling talent are partners in success. They make each other look good. And even the Ultimate Warrior was no exception.

How many of us truly work alone? Even if we telecommute or spend all day in the same cubicle, we most likely work in conjunction with others. Other people are part of all facets of your day-to-day existence, personal life included.

Eventually, you will need somebody's help.

Especially if you have a limited bag of tricks.

While you're running hot, be a gracious partner. Show some gratitude. Collaborate.

Top talent can work with anybody.

Give them a reason to want to work with you.

"I grew up in a very volatile environment. My view was that if I took a beating and lived, I won. I still have that view. It gives me a tremendous advantage because I'm not afraid of failure."

— Vince McMahon

WWE CEO Vince McMahon has done more than anybody in history to invent modern professional wrestling. He is a third-generation wrestling promoter who turned the WWF from a regional, New York-centered wrestling promotion into a global entertainment company. Hulk Hogan, John Cena, Stone Cold Steve Austin, The Ultimate Warrior, Shawn Michaels, Bret Hart, The Undertaker, Brock Lesnar, and The Rock are just a few of the performers who McMahon helped turn into household names, even for people that don't watch wrestling.

As the legend goes, Vince McMahon risked everything he had to make the initial WrestleMania a success. WrestleMania is still going strong over 30 years later, recognized as the Super Bowl equivalent for the sports entertainment industry. However, McMahon has also been part of many failed business ventures, including the football league XFL, the bodybuilding league WBF, the nutritional supplement line ICOPRO, and the WWF restaurant in Times Square.

McMahon's extreme successes have widely surpassed his failures, even the most visible one. He is reportedly a billionaire, and you don't amass that kind of wealth by playing it safe. He could sleep in every day, never lift another finger, and live the rest of his life in opulent comfort. That's not what he wants. McMahon does not coast on past success. Over 70 years old, he still wants to grow and conquer.

And he's never been afraid to show he can take a beating and get back up — in the ring, or in the public arena. He is ready to do everything possible so that he does not fail. Bold, direct, and unflinching, he does not fear failure.

For McMahon, potential failure is not a deterrent. It's a challenge.

No matter what sport, undefeated teams are rare.

If you want to play the game, you will lose.

The fledgling XFL folded in 2001 — but the league is set to return in 2020.

McMahon survived his biggest defeat.

He doesn't let failure stop him.

Will you?

> **"If at first you don't succeed, see if there is a prize for the losers."**
>
> **— Jerry "The King" Lawler**

Wrestling has countless champions. It only has one king: Jerry "The King" Lawler. Many fans and civilians outside of the Memphis territory first learned about Lawler during his feud with comedian Andy Kaufman, a legendary show business story that unfolded over 35 years ago. Lawler's first run with the WWF was over 25 years ago, in which he reinvented himself as a broadcaster.

Amazingly, these days Lawler still wrestles over 50 times a year on the independent circuit. He hosts the *Dinner With the King* podcast. His kingdom includes a pair of restaurants in the Memphis area. He still makes occasional appearances at WWE events and conventions all over the world. Still wrestling royalty, he was one of the hosts of 2018's inaugural Chris Jericho's Rock 'N' Wrestling Rager at Sea. Lawler maintains a top name, with a work ethic which few can match.

The majority of lessons in this book focus on winning and having your eye on the prize. But even Vince McMahon doesn't win every time. As an announcer, Lawler reinvented himself as figure who was still capable of genuine menace, but was more likely to be funny. Here, he makes a joke about not winning.

Losing is never fun.

But it happens.

No one can win everything.

We don't get every job. Some pitches don't land. Try as we might, we won't close every deal. Sometimes it is still rewarding and flattering to finish in second or third place. You don't have to like losing. But you're not serving your future self if you're satisfied being the top loser.

Coming close to victory can still serve as a reminder that you worked hard and you're close to your goal. Apply the same energy and effort to your next pursuit. Remember the sting of the loss. Make it fuel when you need to push harder.

Defeats are temporary — if you keep going and win.

Lords of Discipline author Pat Conroy wrote an entire memoir, *My Losing Season*, exploring the painful truth behind the endlessly-cited bromide, "You learn more from losing than you do from winning." Conroy concludes, "I learned to accept loss as part of natural law. My team taught me there could be courage and dignity and humanity in loss. They taught me how to pull myself up, to hold my head high, and to soldier on."[7]

A loss isn't the end.

Neither is a win.

Work never ends.

A win or loss may make us feel a certain way. If you handle either the right way, what happens next is more important.

> "Don't hunt what you
> can't kill."
>
> — **Shawn Michaels**

Be careful what you wish for. If you head out for a destination, you might get there. And then what are you going to do?

One of — if not the — greatest in-ring performers in the history of professional wrestling, Shawn Michaels worked for over 30 years. As the leader of the D-Generation X stable, he helped change the face of wrestling. The only thing he was unsuccessful at was retiring. Michaels was a four-time world champion, a two-time Royal Rumble winner, and a participant in 11 of *Pro Wrestling Illustrated's Matches Of The Year*. Unsurprisingly, Michaels is an inductee into multiple halls of fame, not just WWE's.

But wrestling was not the quickest or easiest road for Michaels. He debuted in 1984, when WWE was packed with giant wrestlers and painted cartoon-character personas. Michaels' journey to his first world championship was over a decade in the making. He made his name at a time when he was one of the smaller in-ring performers, which made his professional climb steep and slow. Over the years, he overcame substance abuse and a variety of personal problems. More than 20 years after he achieved superstar status, Michaels is still revered both as in-ring performer and a mentor for up-and-coming talent.

Michaels is an active hunter, which expands his library of hard-won knowledge into the realm of life-and-death. In many ways, he has seen ambitions lead adventurers down a dangerous path. Michaels warns us: Don't just plan your way to a goal. Think about what you'll do next.

If you wound a 600-pound wild boar and pin it in a tight spot, the animal may have one final lesson for you.

If you come close to your dreams, will you be ready?

Be aware of what you are pursuing.

Eliminating fear is one thing. But you also should know your limitations before taking a big leap. Otherwise, it can kill you, ending your run in work — or life.

Even if you are not a traditional hunter, keep Michaels' advice in mind when you're setting a goal.

A common dream is to be a rock star. But do you know exactly what that path entails? Writing songs and performing on a stage is only a small part of that job. It's a cutthroat business filled with fatal temptations and legal pitfalls that can drain your lifetime earnings.

In many fields, talent is not enough to achieve and maintain success. Plan beyond your arrival. Whatever your business, learn the business.

Do your homework. Know what you are getting into. Know what you are up against.

"Ever since I came from Italy when I was 15, I had a dream. It was a dream that I never even told my parents about, because I didn't want to be laughed at or thought crazy. My dream was someday to become a professional wrestler, and it was to this goal that I had trained so hard all my life.... When I left work, I would go to the gym for four hours every night and work out, day in day out, week after week, weightlifting, wrestling and waiting for my chance to fulfill my dream."

— Bruno Sammartino

With all respect to Bret Hart, Bruno Sammartino is the best there ever was. To argue otherwise, you need a whole new set of metrics and a much lower bar.

The WWE's obituary[8] for the Hall of Famer ran down a staggering set of statistics, distinctions, and superlatives:

Sammartino was the longest-reigning WWE champion in history. He wore the strap for nearly eight years — 2,803 consecutive days.

As marquee talent, he sold out Madison Square Garden 188 times (and headlined it 211[9]).

He was the first two-time WWE Champion.

He headlined three WWE shows at New York's Shea Stadium.

He was a good guy for his entire career.

Sammartino set a world record for bench press in 1959 (565 pounds, with no steroids or straps[10]).

He made his pro wrestling debut in 1959. He was inducted into the WWE Hall of Fame 50 years after he first won the title. And he was still known, beloved, and respected.

"Nobody deserves to be recognized for being a big star and paving the way for the stars of today more than Bruno," said Triple H when Sammartino finally agreed to join the Hall. "Everything that we have today in the business, Bruno was a cornerstone of that foundation."[11]

Born in Italy, Sammartino eluded Nazi forces that occupied his hometown, Pizzoferrato. When his family immigrated to America, he set some big goals.

Even after surviving a fascist invasion, young Sammartino still knew fear. And it was a big fear, something you can probably relate to: He was afraid to share his dreams with the people around him. What if they knew what he wanted? What if they laughed at him? What if he didn't make it? But Sammartino didn't let fear stop him.

Bruno didn't share his goals with everybody at first. But he did start moving toward them. He wanted to wrestle. So he studied the field. He learned how to do it.

After work, no doubt, he was tired. He probably wanted to take more naps. Or spend some time with his friends. But he wanted something else — and he wanted it more. So after work, he went to work.

Over time, Sammartino transformed himself from a 90-pound undernourished weakling. Through willpower, sweat and determination, he turned himself into a true giant — a massive physical specimen with character to match. He was a legendary family man and role model.

As a young, hungry, aspiring wrestler, Bruno Sammartino didn't wait for a chance; he *prepared* for a chance.

Sammartino made good on his goals in a run that lasted nearly 30 years, until 1987. A decade later, he distanced himself from the WWE during the ribald Attitude Era, citing *Raw*'s raunchy language and sexy storylines.

He was a lock for the Hall of Fame, but refused to associate with the company until it cleaned up its act and elevated back to his standards.

"One of the finest men I knew, in life and in business," Vince McMcahon declared when Sammartino passed.[12] "Bruno Sammartino proved that hard work can overcome even the most difficult of circumstances. He will be missed."

"I'm not afraid to go up to people and pick their brains and ask for advice. To me, that's how you get better. That's how I've gotten better at everything I've ever done. Don't be too proud to ask for help."

— Batista

Dave "Batista" Bautista is one of wrestling's great breakout stories. He grew into a role as a star, showing the world he was everything they thought he was — and so much more.

He first entered the wrestling world in the late 1990s, after years studying martial arts and working as a bouncer. After a feud with The Rock, he really took off with the launch of the Evolution stable in 2003, where he worked alongside Ric Flair, Triple H and fellow up-and-comer Randy Orton. Ultimately, Batista would have four reigns as WWE's World Heavyweight Champion, in addition to other titles.

In 2010, Batista left WWE to pursue other projects, including MMA fighting and a career in Hollywood.

In short order, he became a reliable scene-stealing presence in a variety of high-profile film projects, including *Guardians of the Galaxy*, *Blade Runner 2049* and *Riddick*.

When Batista made a short-term return to WWE in 2013, it was entirely on his own terms. Nowadays, Batista is not only starring in movies, but also serving as a producer on some of those films. The WWE welcomes him back with open arms, as they do for Dwayne "The Rock" Johnson; Batista was an honored guest as part of *Raw 1000*, the 1,000th episode of *Raw*.

Batista readily admits he strategizes before making big moves. And he doesn't pretend he is working from his own playbook. He realizes there is much to learn from others, even if he has a unique combination of aptitudes, gifts and circumstances — as we all do. Even though he was successful in one arena, he realizes he doesn't know everything.

It's a common phenomenon among doctors, lawyers, engineers, and highly educated people: They're usually the smartest person in the room. So they assume they're always the smartest person in the room. And you can't tell them anything.

A humble attitude like Batista's can prevent costly mistakes. Improvement is a gradual process.

Even if you are not a movie star or main-event wrestler, this advice applies to just about every facet of life. One brief piece of advice from a veteran can save you years of trial and error.

Almost everything has been done or experienced by someone, so why not ask people how they handled particular situations?

Maybe they'll say no. If they do, you'll live.

Maybe they'll give you one piece of useful information that opens doors.

And then perhaps you can find another person to ask for their two cents.

People are proud of what they know. They like to talk about it.

Make every conversation a lesson.

Asking for advice helps you strategize. Then you get learn how to go where want to be, moving further, faster.

Shayna Baszler (left) knees Dakota Kai. By Ed Battes.

"Sometimes, half the fun is failing. Learning from your mistakes, waking up the next morning, and saying 'Okay. Watch out. Here I come again. A little bit smarter, licking my wounds, and really not looking forward to getting my ass kicked the way I just did yesterday.' So now, I'm just a little more dangerous."

— Paul Heyman

Paul Heyman is one of the great minds — and mouths — in the history of wrestling. The business has never seen anybody quite like him.

Other people have been successful promoters with their own wrestling companies. Other behind-the-scenes geniuses have been head writers. Other on-screen managers have taken an occasional bump during a match. But few have done of all those jobs simultaneously — certainly not as well, on such a high level, as Paul "Paul E. Dangerously" Heyman.

Heyman is best known for masterminding the iconoclastic, extreme, and boundary-shattering ECW, which was ultimately purchased by WWE after a meteoric rise led to insurmountable financial woes. (Again, we are reminded: Success can be more dangerous than failure.) Heyman has worked for WWE in various capacities.

After decades in the spotlight, Heyman's abilities are widely known and well documented — yet he still has the amazing ability to keep people guessing. Even when he is doing an interview, while seeming to be out-of-character, he can provide breezy responses that seem honest and personalized. But he is always able to work in his promotional know-how and avoid discussing the things he wishes to keep to himself. A master rhetorician, he manages to be relatable, without ever stopping the show.

Like McMahon, Heyman knows that failure is inevitable. You are bound to make mistakes. If you honestly assess your performance, you learn from your mistakes. With the right mindset, in fact, failing can be fun.

If you can shift your perspective and keep a positive point of view, you are likely to feel less pressure about needing to deliver immediate results. If you feel like you have nothing to lose, you have nothing to fear.

Every business has stories about somebody who was nearly broke, on their last legs, and about to meet failure head on. With nothing to lose, they relaxed and tried one last gambit that seemed like a longshot — but a fun one. They decided to go out in style. And that one last fearless gambit turned the company's fortunes around.

Sometimes that last gambit isn't a rebirth. Sometimes you do, in fact, go with a smile.

Most people like a smile.

Heyman built an internationally respected brand in ECW. It was his life's work. It went bankrupt. Sometimes you catch a bad break. Business is tough. Even after his great creation folded, Heyman remained a respected top name in the business.

Positive attitudes are magnetic. If you bring a vocally optimistic approach to a task, you are more likely to come across as likable. If people like you, they are more likely to cooperate.

Few people who are immediately successful maintain long-term success.

Failing today may be the key to success tomorrow.

And if you survive, how will you respond?

Will you be broken?

Or glad to be alive?

Mark Henry. Photo courtesy of WWE & Ricky Media.

> **"You can't tell people what to do if you're a failure... You have to be responsible, and you've got to lead by example."**
>
> **— Mark Henry**

The behemoth Mark Henry is a two-time U.S. Olympian, a Pan American Games medalist, a three-time U.S. National Weightlifting Champion, and holder of several world records that still stand. As a professional wrestler, he was a multi-time World Heavyweight Champion and a 2018 inductee into the WWE Hall of Fame. Henry was also enshrined in the International Sports Hall of Fame in 2012.

Henry is a professional senser of potential. While Henry is retired from athletic competition, he is still active. He continues working with the WWE as an ambassador, which includes recruiting new talent. Henry is pursuing a number of film and television projects. He also co-hosts the popular SiriusXM show *Busted Open Radio*. A recent episode of the Facebook Watch series *Risky Biz* showcased yet another side of the versatile performer.

Henry believes in leading by example.

Any pencil-neck can be in charge, bark orders at people, and treat them badly. It takes a professional to set a tone for an organization, a leader. Often, the best managers can teach their employees to achieve because they have been there and done that. Your team will work harder if they know you're willing to match — or exceed — their effort.

Henry preaches overall responsibility. You need to own up to your actions.

Finally, he distinguishes between failing and being a failure.

The definition of a "failure" is up for debate. Some will argue a person who has given their all to accomplish a goal has not failed.

In fields that involve creativity and risk, you cannot guarantee how your work will be received, and whether it will find an audience.

If you don't do your best work, you have failed… to prepare.

You cannot control results.

You can only control how much effort you exert.

The way you work creates credibility and respect.

If people know you give your all, they are more likely to accept your advice, your requests, your guidance, your input, your management.

For your money, what is the difference between failure and not achieving the desired outcome?

What do *you* think constitutes failure?

"Common sense tells you how to do things. And people don't really follow that."

— Salina de la Renta

At this point, rising star Salina de la Renta is one of the focal points of Major League Wrestling. In some of her earliest matches, de la Renta worked alongside Santana Garrett, Thea Trinidad (now WWE's Zelina Vega), and former TNA Knockout Raquel.

Common sense is hard to define, but it's important. And it makes the difference in any career, whether you're a teacher or a waiter. Especially if you have to deal with people. And wrestling is a people business.

In a world where everyone has to think about branding and online promotion and HR guidelines and tough bottom-line financial decisions, common sense may be uncommon.

We know common sense when we see it — if we have common sense. Some people are born with it. Some develop it through hard-won experience.

On one level, common sense is a mental flow state that allows us to read a situation without overthinking it. People with common sense instinctively understand the interconnected factors of a situation.

Decisions based in common sense don't just consider what is *possible* in a situation; they factor in human emotions.

Managers with common sense consider how different options might make the people involved feel. If we're making responsible decisions, a sound judgment call will factor in the human cost of a decision.

People who lack common sense might not be able to understand other people's feelings.

They might not be able to understand their own.

When you have a decision to make, sometimes the answer is as simple as assessing the situation and considering how it will make you feel. Malcolm Gladwell — a keen observer of human dynamics, and author of influential books including *The Tipping Point* — calls this phenomenon The Blink Response: Everything you know about a situation gives you an overall *feeling* about it. "Intuition" is a plainer word for it.

Maybe an opportunity has a big potential gain. But you have a bad feeling about it.

Maybe an opportunity has a big potential loss. But you have a good feeling about it.

You know how you feel.

You know what you want to do.

You should know a bad deal when you see one.

If you trust that feeling, you might make a snap decision about the best course of action, a decision in the blink of an eye.

Countless wrestlers had their big breakthrough when they embraced a course of action only they understood. Everybody else told them to follow the company's lead, to do what the bosses recommended, to use a traditional approach. But they sensed an opportunity, an option that *felt* better.

That *better* feeling came from common sense.

Part II:

On Wrestling

"The average person has no problem suspending their disbelief for Bruce Willis in *Die Hard*. But the fact that wrestling is sort of live and came out of this carnival culture, it's sort of this tainted thing. I'm constantly trying to explain to people what I find fascinating about professional wrestling and why it's a high art form."

— Billy Corgan

That Billy Corgan? Yes, that Billy Corgan. Beyond selling over 30 million albums as the leader of The Smashing Pumpkins — which remains an arena-level act decades after forming — Corgan is one of wrestling's most visible, famous fans. This passion led him to purchase the storied National Wrestling Alliance, after decades of dabbling around the business.

Corgan's passion for wrestling goes back to his childhood, but he reportedly lapsed as a fan after music became his top passion. Corgan ultimately came back to wrestling when he accidentally discovered ECW on late-night television. He later got involved in an ECW storyline or two. Before Paul Heyman sold ECW to WWE, he tried to sell it to Corgan.

Here, Corgan is discussing the history of professional wrestling, which has roots in the American carnival circuit. To him, wrestling is a true art form, "high art" that is as legitimate as any other theatrical or dramatic production. It is as refined and involved as an opera, a Michelin-starred chef's kitchen creation or paintings in a museum. However, the average person may look down on wrestling while celebrating and suspending disbelief for an obviously fictional action movie.

If you are a wrestling fan, you have undoubtedly heard from other people that wrestling is "fake." Or that they used to like it. Or any number of other condescending viewpoints that marginalize it.

Corgan has the correct perspective on the discipline. It's one of the great and distinctly American art forms, like jazz and stand-up comedy. Wrestling may not be for everybody; it's violent drama. But drama it is, like *Twilight*, *Pitch Perfect*, or any other work of fiction that has babyfaces and heels.

Should wrestling be considered somehow inferior to other versions of storytelling?

Not if you like art. And really understand it.

> "To most people, wrestling is a laughingstock. But fortunately, I'm reaching people who otherwise wouldn't watch it."
>
> — Andy Kaufman

Similar to Billy Corgan, Andy Kaufman found international success as a iconic entertainer, then parlayed that fame into a stint in wrestling. Kaufman was the subject of the biopic *Man on the Moon* — as portrayed by Jim Carrey — which covered his whole life and career, including his work with *Saturday Night Live, Late Night With David Letterman,* and *Taxi.* But it was Kaufman's work within the Memphis wrestling territory that leveled him up from beloved comedian to entertainment legend.

At the height of his fame, Kaufman spent time in Memphis, feuding with Jerry "The King" Lawler. Playing the heel, he mocked the people of Tennessee, bragging what a big star he was in Hollywood. The reality was that Kaufman was originally from Long Island, New York. But his involvement in wrestling created the template for a prefab storyline.

In Kaufman's case, the narrative was the story of an obnoxious superstar blustering into the wrestling world. He insulted its fans, disrespected its traditions, called out its champion, and questioned its integrity — all the while playing into its well-established conventions.

When he entered Memphis, Kaufman was actually staging one of wrestling's most exciting conventions, the ever-popular invasion angle: A star from an outside territory arrives in town. He declares war on the establishment. He pretends to be an outsider. But he's working of the same company, a partner with the established fan favorites.

David Arquette, Kevin Federline and Dennis Rodman are Hollywood invaders who have been welcomed into that storyline's starring role over the last two decades. But Kaufman and Lawler's angle so thoroughly blurred the line between reality and performance that fans on both sides howled for blood, grew confused, and turned away. Even though Kaufman represented the entirely fabricated world of televised fiction, his mainstream fans weren't amused by his turn as a wrestling heel.

Kaufman, like Corgan, acknowledged that many people see wrestling as low-brow entertainment.

But like ballet and the symphony, wrestling requires patrons and promoters.

Kaufman also invested his money, time, and credibility, hoping to make the art more respectable to the average consumer.

Did fans on either side appreciate Kaufman's patronage?

No.

Did they enjoy it?

They did watch.

Was it popular?

It did take Lawler from a regional program and put him on David Letterman's network TV show.

Did it work?

Fans on both sides booed Kaufman and Lawler off the screen.

And we're still talking about it.

> "I think drugs and alcohol aren't a wrestling problem, it's a life problem, it's a people problem."
>
> — CM Punk

The iconoclastic WWE champion CM Punk also blurred the line between reality and wrestling, in a way that changed the business. In 2011, he spun backstage politics and his onscreen persona into a masterful promo called "The Pipe Bomb," which was later named the no. 2 moment in the history of Raw. The big show hadn't seen anyone quite like him before. And it hasn't seen anyone like him since.

One of the longest-reigning WWE Champions of the modern era, CM Punk often called himself "The Best in the World." (And so did others.) Like Kevin Owens, Punk is another performer who helped redefine how a wrestler looks and acts. And years after his departure, WWE crowds still chant his name at live events.

Punk abruptly left the WWE in 2014. More than any grappler in the history of wrestling, Punk created an in-ring character based on his real-life persona. If the human being behind CM Punk was not living the lifestyle preached by the character of CM Punk, you certainly never heard about it. When punk called out the WWE's corrupt, socially reinforced power structure, he felt it in his bones.

Punk took his stage name from punk-rock culture. His character was rooted in a subset of it: the straight-edge movement. Straight-edge punks rejected drugs, alcohol, cigarettes and all recreational chemicals. Punk billed himself as the "Straight-Edge Superstar." From era to era, other wrestlers have promoted themselves as clean-living upright citizens, including Daniel Bryan, Lanny Poffo and longtime champion Bob Backlund. When the pure-hearted all-American boys get a push, it serves a very real function for the business. It broadcasts the message, "The best of us are good guys." And not for nothing.

On screen, the scientific golden boys are seldom humble about their lifestyle. Punk famously cited his straightedge status to explain why he was "better" than other wrestlers. He genuinely believed this, too. For good reason.

Wrestling's stigmas include stereotypes. The business has had a series of scandals and premature deaths, many of them fueled by the use and abuse of alcohol and drugs. Those rare scandals cast a shadow on the rest of the wrestlers, casting them as hard-partying wasteoids. In the public eye, Punk's profession and persona are diminished because, according to the stereotype, "Wrestlers party."

And when someone else's behavior smudges Punk's carefully cultivated wholesome image, he takes it personally.

And, as in the "Pipe Bomb" promo, Punk's frustration is rooted in reality.

Stereotypes are stereotypes.

Some wrestlers drink.

So do some nurses.

So do some forestry experts.

Some people use drugs and alcohol.

Some of them are wrestlers.

They don't do it because they're wrestlers.

They do it because they're the kind of people who drink or use drugs.

So when you think you know someone, *do* you know them?

Or are you thinking about somebody like them?

And is that a fair, respectful way to think about somebody else who makes a living in a demanding business?

Velveteen Dream (left) drops a double axehandle on Aleister Black. By Ed Battes.

"Every critic I've ever had, they weren't wrestlers. Every wrestler I've ever had critique me, they were always into my stuff or what I'm doing out there. For a non-wrestler, someone who doesn't even know how to lock up... for them to critique any of us, it really does pop me."

— Roman Reigns

Roman Reigns is the latest in a long chain of wrestling royalty, a notable part of the Anoi'i dynasty of Samoa. The dynasty's wrestlers include The Rock, The Usos, Tamina, and Yokozuna. His father is Sika of The Wild Samoans. His brother wrestled as Rosey of 3-Minute Warning, alongside cousin Jamal (later known as Umaga).

Roman Reigns is a multi-time WWE World Heavyweight Champion and former Universal Champion, United States Champion, Intercontinental Champion and WWE Tag Team Champion. As a Triple Crown and Grand Slam Champion, Reigns is one of the few wrestlers to headline multiple WrestleManias. But that does not mean that Reigns has always been cheered, even when working as a babyface. He creates reactions, some positive, some negative, some appreciative, some uninformed.

In this quote, Reigns addresses armchair critics, idle viewers who criticize his performance when he's in the hard-earned position under the spotlight.

By Reigns' estimation, most of those haters are themselves not wrestlers and not as "smart" as they think — in the culture of wrestling, the word "smart" applies to fans who are educated about the business, who understand and appreciate its machinations. Smart fans believe their opinions are not only informed, but elevated.

In Reigns' professional opinion, someone sitting at home on a sofa has not earned the right to assess his performance. They haven't been inside the machine. So from outside, they don't understand how it works. The mere fact that they are vocally negative proves that he is good at his job. He isn't worried about what the haters think; he is too busy achieving something.

And in Reigns' case, he truly put more effort into his performance than even the biggest, smartest fans could have guessed. In late 2018, Reigns shocked the world by relinquishing the WWE Universal

Championship, for a very real reason. He had been living and wrestling with a devastating health problem that had finally been diagnosed: leukemia. And it wasn't the first time. In an emotional promo, he revealed he had first been diagnosed with the blood cancer at the age of 22. And now it had returned.

And that is the grappler internet warriors found unworthy of his role in the company.

More than ever, it seemed their experience wasn't a useful reference for his fortitude.

This dynamic applies to you, no matter your industry for employment. If someone takes the time to negatively critique your work, consider the source. If someone tells you your movie script stinks, consider how many scripts they have written. If they don't like your business plan, how many companies have they successfully founded?

Naysayers often resent your ability to start and finish a project you mentioned. They are sitting around, reacting to something you created. They haven't risked anything. They haven't created anything. They are not helping you.

Maybe your work isn't perfect. But you did it. You made something. You did something.

First we learn to do something. Then we learn to do it well.

Everybody's work has room for improvement. We can all benefit from some input.

Chase Oliver hits a shooting star on Magnum CK. By Ed Battes.

"Pro wrestling is not fake;
it's sports entertainment.
We go out there and we
perform. And a lot of
what we do out there
is real.... There is a
predetermined winner...
[But] the fans don't
know who it is. And
that's what makes it so
intriguing."

— Kurt Angle

Most wrestling greats have been the champion of their company. Many of those same performers crossed over into the mainstream culture, and now they're recognizable names to people who never saw them in the squared circle. But only one pro wrestler has been decorated as the ultimate amateur wrestler: U.S. Olympic gold medalist Kurt Angle.

Angle is one of the first success stories of the WWE developmental system. He was signed by 1998. He made his way onto WWF television in 1999. After more than 10 years away, Angle returned to the WWE in 2017, not only to be inducted into the

WWE Hall of Fame, but also to serve as the general manager of *Monday Night Raw*. Since then, Angle has wrestled as part of some major matches. Over 20 years after turning pro, he is still a fan favorite.

Here, Angle is addressing an industry-shaking paradigm shift by referring to wrestling as "sports entertainment." He is also openly referring to what was once a well-kept secret: the fact that each match, unlike most sporting events, will end with "a predetermined winner." But he also acknowledges that many aspects of wrestling are "real," even though it is part of a performance.

Angle's quote teaches an important lesson: In wrestling, as in the rest of life, things are not simply black or white. Two different things may be true simultaneously without negating each other. One quality does not erase another.

Wrestling is not fully "real," yet it is not "fake." A match may be a choreographed routine with a predetermined winner. But the ending does not negate the hours of cardio training that preceded a match. A predetermined ending does not eliminate the bone-crunching impact of a flying headbutt.

Personally and professionally, many things you will encounter may be commonly recognized as a clear-cut issue. Yet there may be more going on, beyond what is visible from the outside.It may be wise to reserve judgment.

If you think a predetermined outcome means wrestling isn't "real," you're fundamentally misunderstanding the art you're consuming.

And if you're wrong about that issue, what else might you be wrong about?

> # "Wrestling is ballet with violence."

> ## — Jesse Ventura

Former Minnesota governor Jesse "The Body" Ventura first served his country as a Navy SEAL, a legendarily elite military special operations force. He later found fame as a pro wrestler. He has since been best-selling author and Hollywood actor. To put it mildly, he is a substantial person with a diverse skill set. If not for wrestling, we might not know his name.

If you are a long-term WWE fan, odds are that you remember Ventura more for his color commentary than his in-ring performances. As an announcer, Ventura cultivated an innovative heel persona that was not only effective, but helped create a template for color commentary within wrestling. Ventura generally sided with fellow heels. He was always quick with one-liners, suiting his sardonic persona. Meanwhile, his babyface foil — usually Vince McMahon or Gorilla Monsoon — would reinforce why we should be cheering for the good guy to win. Ventura's argument was always a lot more entertaining. Verbal skills will take you far. Between his WWF run and politics, Ventura provided commentary for WCW.

Like ballet, wrestling requires a superhuman level of grace and toughness developed over years of physically demanding, painful preparation. Wrestling is a choreographed routine, but the plot is a fight. Watch the rehearsal footage on reality hit *Dancing With the Stars* — it is very close to actual wrestling: Each couple has a leader who calls what will be happen. Without that designated leader or structure, the performance would not offer a flowing storyline or narrative.

Think about how much blood, sweat, pain, and time your least favorite WWE wrestler had to invest before they could even claim a spot in an untelevised, pre-*Raw* dark match.

How does this violent ballet apply to you?

At a professional level, most presentations require incalculable training and experience, whether they're an improv routine, a wedding toast, or a PowerPoint presentation. And in most productions, the participants need to cooperate and fulfill roles.

Sometimes you lead. Sometimes you follow.

Sometimes you need to endure peril, pain and danger if you want to put on a memorable, undeniable performance. The audience will forget everybody who played it safe.

Sometimes you support. Sometimes you're the star.

Sometimes you're backstage, unseen, unheard.

Every role is important.

As The Rock said many a time: Know your role.

> "Your body has this instinct to start healing. And then you go back to work, and it hurts even more. It's almost better to keep your body messed-up."
>
> — Gail Kim

Gail Kim is one of the most celebrated female wrestlers of all-time. She won the WWE Women's Championship in her first match. She earned that stellar debut as the record-setting seven-time TNA / Impact Knockouts Champion. She was the first female inductee in the TNA Hall of Fame.

Kim appears to be retired as an in-ring performer — granted, she did announce her retirement while being recognized as the TNA Knockouts Champion. Kim wrestled until she was nearly 41. And she is still very involved within the wrestling business. Beyond signings and the occasional on-screen appearance, she is a producer and agent for Impact Wrestling. Furthermore, as the wife of celebrity chef Robert Irvine, Kim also pops up in the food world.

Kim's quote is about pain and momentum: The human body — and mind — can adjust to almost anything. When your body feels "messed-up" or sore on a long-term basis, it can feel less painful to just keep plowing ahead with that pain. Some things only hurt when you stop moving long enough to let them.

But the world offers us many kinds of pain.

A productive, remarkable life is seldom comfortable.

In the self-help movement, one of the great clichés is "get outside your comfort zone."

If you're comfortable and just repeating things you have done before, you're probably not doing anything new, exciting, and groundbreaking.

Being comfortable won't get you anywhere.

The Yes Theory clothing and lifestyle brand has an entire line designed around the slogan "seek discomfort."

If you consistently go out of your way to face uncomfortable situations, everything else you do will seem easier.

You will learn to do new things.

You will learn to perform under pressure.

Kim's mindset applies to any situation in which you don't feel like doing something.

Maybe you're comfortable and warm in a nice soft bed.

Maybe you don't want to wake up early, get out of bed, exercise or start a new project. Your body might tell you, "I'm tired." You might agree.

But if you can just start, the rest is easier. Some pain goes away when you warm up.

Keep pushing ahead a little bit further every day.

Think of every action as a small step in your long-term journey.

And you will never reap the benefits of that journey if you quit. And certainly won't arrive if you don't start in the first place.

Don't let discomfort stop you.

> "A live performance is the same no matter what genre it is. Wrestling, rock 'n roll, hosting, acting — it's the same thing."
>
> — Chris Jericho

More than 25 years after breaking into the wrestling business, Chris Jericho is still a main-event talent.

Over that amazingly long career, he has held major titles from New Japan Pro-Wrestling's Intercontinental belt to the WWE Heavyweight Championship. And he has squared off in notable feuds and matches with some of the legends of the ring, including The Rock, Stone Cold Steve Austin, Hulk Hogan, Ric Flair, Shawn Michaels and just about every important wrestler of the 1990s, 2000s and 2010s.

Yet wrestling is only one facet of Jericho's success. After he takes his bumps, he doesn't sleep in, rest, and recuperate. He stays in motion. He fronts the headliner rock band Fozzy. He is a prolific podcaster who also heads up the Jericho Network, producing other podcasts, partnering with the Westwood One communications company. He has written four memoirs. He has also worked extensively as an actor and television host. In his spare time, he staged his own themed cruise, Chris Jericho's Rock 'N' Wrestling Rager at Sea.

To Jericho, performing is performing. If you can perform well in one particular media, genre or area, you likely have what it takes to do well in another form, style, or discipline. Jericho sees his role as an overall entertainer and live performer, not just a professional wrestler.

Like Jericho, you can use your skills as building blocks for a bigger, better, richer life.

If you have the creative know-how to tell a good joke, why can't you level up and deliver a moving speech?

If you can prepare a speech, you can write an article, a book, a short story or a joke.

If you have the ability to improvise on a guitar, why can't you improvise in other areas of your life?

If you can do one thing well, don't stop there. You can probably do another. And another.

Do yourself a favor and solidify your performance skills, because — as Shakespeare wrote — "All the world's a stage."

You can live comfortably if you're quiet and you enjoy puzzles.

But if you want to be noticed, learn how to entertain, stage a production, and put on a show.

Diamond Dallas Page earned tremendous recognition outside of wrestling, yet he remains relevant in the business, an influential presence beyond his 2017 WWE Hall of Fame induction.

DDP not only pops up from time to time on WWE programming, but he was part of last year's game-changing All In event in Chicago and a featured guest on Chris Jericho's cruise. DDP is the kind of elite wrestling legend that easily bridges the gap between the old and the new.

Reality television has been around for decades, but it became a permanent genre in the United States in the early 2000s, a staple of network and niche television programming with popularity to rival the most elaborate, expensive Hollywood productions. Unlike wrestling and ballet, reality TV looks deceptively simple.

Many of the better unscripted — and apparently spontaneous — shows actually star people who used to be on scripted shows. They look like shoots. They're really works. Everything is a work.

DDP identifies wrestling as a progenitor of the "reality television" concept, since it blurs the line between its fictional and non-fictional components. When watching wrestling, we know the outcome is predetermined and that the performers are acting — even if folks like John Cena, Kurt Angle, Randy

Orton, Jeff Hardy and Brock Lesnar are using their real names when performing.

But we do not know everything that is going to happen. And we can't always tell when the performers are making mistakes. And we don't know when those mistakes will become happy accidents that redirect a story — or the business itself — into an exciting new direction.

If you are watching TV or reading a newspaper, odds are you are consuming a narrative: Somebody is telling you a story.

Maybe someone wrote that story, invented it, concocted it, fabricated it.

Maybe a team of producers collected a select series of facts and factors about a situation. And then they told it back to you, presenting an incomplete recreation, a short version.

Stories are easier to sell — and tell — if they follow a conventional narrative. Audiences are more likely to understand a recognizable story we can relate to and understand: Maybe an underdog defeats an established opponent. A good guy struggles against a corrupt bad guy. An outspoken figure falls from grace and struggles to regain integrity. A principled hero babyface wrestles a shifty heel who will use every dirty trick to cheat their way to an undeserved victory.

Decades before *Survivor*, wrestling promoters realized people want to see colorful characters compete in exotic locations, in heightened circumstances. We're more invested when the situation has a winner and loser. We'll stay tuned moment to moment if somebody might say something shocking. Stakes are high if somebody might get hurt.

Screenwriters, producers, and even journalists hammer stories into preconceived narratives. They present a new story in the shape of one we already know. Often, they do it at the expense of truth and accuracy.

So think about everything you read or see, from reported news to gossip. If someone is telling you a story, they are leaving out some details. Sometimes the people being portrayed as the "good guys" are actually the opposite, and vice versa.

Don't believe everything you hear.

Don't believe everything you see.

Things are not often as they seem.

Especially when other people have creative control.

Britt Baker (right) and Karen Q. By Ed Battes.

> "I never thought I was a bad person. I just thought I was the one good person living in a world of bad people."

> — Dean Ambrose

Dean Ambrose became a world-class star as one third of the all-star faction The Shield. Prior to landing on the WWE roster, Ambrose was a well-traveled competitor with a dozen title reigns, wrestling as Jon Moxley. He has since become the WWE's youngest Grand Slam Champion, headlined more than his share of pay-per-views, worn a half-dozen belts, and been named *Pro Wrestling Illustrated*'s Most Popular Wrestler of the Year for two consecutive years.

Ambrose's microphone skills made him a standout. Whether working babyface or heel, he presents himself as an unstable character, making fans believe his internal chaos might erupt at any minute. Ambrose cuts philosophical promos that unite the storyline, wrestlers, company and fans into participants in one epic story.

Until recently, Ambrose portrayed a mean-spirited heel. Sulking, he posed and insulted the crowd, citing their lack of both hygiene and sophistication.

Ambrose has an exceptional grip on not just storytelling psychology, but psychology itself: Heels do not think of themselves as heels. Even if they are the only person with their mindset, bad guys may think of themselves as fighting for what they perceive as good.

Everybody is the hero of their own story. Nobody goes through the day imagining they're making the world a worse place.

Think of every public apology statement you've ever heard: Nobody ever says, "I was doing terrible things. People like me are a problem. It's a good thing somebody stopped me."

When someone is involved in something so controversial it requires a public apology, the statement always explains why they were, in fact, in the right — and pursuing admirable goals.

Apply that dynamic to everyday working life. Just about every office, team or family has a person that makes everybody else roll their eyes.

Try to think of a coworker who is hard to deal with, who makes the product and atmosphere worse. Imagine a teammate who is happy to list problems, but never offers solutions — and somehow remains on the payroll.

How to deal with the heel in your life?

Lace up the office heel's wrestling boots and walk a mile in them.

See where their heel is coming from. What do they want? Imagine what they have to deal with in their position. Their performance and attitude may be the result of circumstances you don't see.

If you can understand your teammates' motivations and desires, maybe you can cultivate some harmony to replace today's discord.

To be a better co-worker, look to Dean Ambrose. Let him be a lesson in empathy.

> **"If the WWF was about talent, Taka Michinoku would have been WWF champion."**
>
> **— Mick Foley**

Taka Michinoku was not a WWF champion.

You might not even know his name.

Talented though he was.

If you're reading this, you very likely do recognize Mick Foley's name. He was a long-running fan favorite who worked under distinct styles and personas, including the brutal Cactus Jack, the dubiously suave Dude Love, and the bloody, bizarre — and sometimes comic — Mankind.

No matter which character you know him as, Foley is one of wrestling's all-time most beloved performers.

Foley defied all odds on every level: Without a classic physique, he still became a world champion by wrestling in brutal matches that network television often did not broadcast.

After sacrificing his body in the ring for decades, he staged a happy ending, retiring as an in-ring performer while still popular, then continuing to make appearances for WWE, while parlaying his wrestling renown into a second career as an in-demand author and stand-up comic.

You can't say he hasn't earned every bit of success, though you may agree he's an overachiever. He barely got called up to the big show.

As the legend goes: Jim Ross recruited Foley to the WWF. Vince McMahon was not a fan of Foley. The boss did not envision him as a top draw, TV star, and longtime marquee name.

But Foley regularly delivered when he was called upon. His first WWF championship victory was one of WWF's first victories over WCW in the ratings battle known as the Monday Night Wars. Later, Foley helped *Raw* set new record ratings highs, with a segment featuring himself and The Rock, called This Is Your Life.

Taka Michinoku was the first-ever WWF Light Heavyweight Champion. He was notably part of a Japan-centric stable called Kai En Tai, which often showcased Michinoku's comedic side.

Foley has felt the weight of the promotion grinding him down. He survived and came out on top, beating longshot odds. He succeeded because he understands the politics, performance issues, and intangible qualities that make talent reliable in management's eyes.

Talent is not necessarily the top priority of the WWE, which explains why wrestlers have been held back from top positions. Michinoku and countless other performers were far more talented than TV audiences ever realized.

In wrestling and beyond, talent alone will not make you a star in your company.

At a company, the person with the highest rank or the biggest salary or best smile is not necessarily the most talented person there. Performance abilities are an entirely different skill from management abilities. Management skills are entirely different from communication skills. People with unmatched technical skill or knowledge may have an abrasive personality.

If you can't communicate and demonstrate your value to management, your bosses will never take a chance on you. Far more often than not, managers are paid to make safe decisions. Management bets on people who create value. Managers promote people who create value. Managers value people who exceed expectations. If you're not entering your manager's awareness as a competent, confident professional who exceeds the company's needs, somebody else is.

Michinoku rose to Light Heavyweight Champion.

And he rose no further.

Once you think you've arrived, only one person is truly invested in seeing you achieve your full potential. Only one person has an incentive to see you achieve your full potential, to turn your talent into accomplishments: you.

If you want move up the corporate ladder, work on more than your craft.

Jericho raging at sea, against Marty Scurll.
Photo by Will Byington, courtesy Sixthman.

"You should be able to have good matches against anybody."

—Charlie Haas

If you can't do something all the time, on demand, even without your usual preparation and material, you can't *really* do it.

In his 15-plus years as a professional wrestler, Charlie Haas had been multiple-time tag team champion in both the WWE and Ring of Honor. In 2003, he ranked at no. 25 on the PWI 500 list of *Pro Wrestling Illustrated*, the magazine long regarded as the objective bible of the business.

Haas stood out as a financial whiz both before and after life as a wrestler. He was a Goldman Sachs stockbroker before signing with the WWE. Since retiring from the ring, Haas has returned to the corporate world.

If you're truly good at your job, you should be able to do it under difficult circumstances.

If wrestling really is comparable to a dance, all participants have to work in sync with one another. If one of the wrestlers is less skilled than another, the person taking charge should still be able to lead the match efficiently, so that everyone is pulling their weight.

No matter whether it's a committee in your office, a recreational soccer team or a pot-luck dinner, anything requiring collaboration is going to involve one person who is more naturally skilled than some others.

Even if you're a one-man army, the other members of your team still have resources to offer.

Personal excellence is not leadership.

A true leader leads their entire team to victories.

If you're a Lucha wrestler who specializes in aerial maneuvers, but your opponent can't execute high-flying moves, you'd be foolish and dangerous to ask them to operate at a higher level. If you're dedicated to putting on a good show, you will think of another use for their talents.

Don't set your team up for failure.

Figure out what the less-skilled members are capable of doing well. Find a use for that.

If a mission fails while you're the leader, make no mistake: You have failed.

A strong leader should make their team look good.

> "Only in pro wrestling can a company threaten legal action on you, but then probably offer you a job a year later."

> — The Young Bucks

Few wrestling tag teams are as universally loved and respected as The Young Bucks, real-life brothers Matt and Nick Jackson. This forward-thinking tag team may be able to stand toe-to-toe against the WWE itself. They have locked up before.

The Jackson are two of the key players — and minds — behind both the pivotal All In event and the new All Elite Wrestling promotion. They entered the business in the early 2000s. A 21st century sense of media savvy made them superstars.

The Young Bucks' grassroots approach to marketing incorporated interactive social media, including the popular *Being the Elite* web series. Their well-distributed merchandise had something for everyone, including a children's book. They even had their own theme song, recorded by their father, "Papa Buck" Matthew Lee Massie.

The Bucks put themselves on a world-class stage without the help of the WWE. OK; maybe the WWE helped a little bit. But it didn't mean to.

The Jacksons re-popularized the Too Sweet hand gesture the NWO had used during their phenomenal 1990s — only to be hit with a now-infamous cease-and-desist letter from the WWE, which owned the WCW legacy.

The entrepreneurial brothers not only turned that incident into popular merchandise, but into a new hand-gesture known as One Sweet, which they did control. Like true champions, they stared down a situation that would made the average person back down in fear. And they emerged from the challenge victorious, with bigger and brighter star power.

The Young Bucks' quote directly references the WWE's cease-and-desist letter. It also mentions how the WWE "probably" would offer them employment — which was a correct prediction. Before All Elite Wrestling launched, the WWE did attempt to woo them with a remarkably generous contract. This is not the first time the WWE has had an issue with a wrestler, only to later wind up in business together because both parties could make money together, moving forward, doing what was best for business.

You don't need to love everyone you work with, so long as their contributions are somehow beneficial to your overall cause.

That approach applies a "Never say never" approach. Friends often become enemies. Enemies become friends.

Things change.

Especially when money is on the line.

The only constant in the world is change.

You don't have to like it.

But it happens.

"It's often said you don't choose who you fall in love with, which I believe to be true. I also believe you don't choose what you fall in love with."
— Daniel Bryan

Daniel Bryan has something to please fans of just about any generation. He has technical prowess that would appeal to a follower of old-school giant Lou Thesz. He can do the high-risk, fast-paced maneuvers of Lucha. He also spent a lot of time in Japan, so he can perform strong-style in-ring work as well. Those elements all add up to the Daniel Bryan style, which is hard to define — but from any angle, his matches are a thing of artistry.

Bryan wanted to be a professional wrestler since he was a child. Unlike many high-profile recruits, Bryan entered the company as a seasoned in-ring veteran. When Bryan starred in the *NXT* reality series, the company played up his considerable ring time, promoting him as having more experience than his on-screen mentor, The Miz. While part of NXT, Bryan was allowed to move the WWE's big arena shows. He complained, but not because he wanted more time in the spotlight. Instead, what he really wanted was the opportunity to express himself creatively in the ring, at the highest level. He got there.

In his 2015 autobiography *Yes: My Improbable Journey to the Main Event of WrestleMania*, Bryan refers to wrestling as his "love." He views wrestling as part of his destiny. It immediately clicked with him.

So think about what — and not just who — you love.

What drew you in?

Who else shares that love?

What is your goal for that love you feel? Do you want to feel it? Share it? Spread it around?

What do you want to do on this Earth?

Do you want to be someone who makes the world a better place, using the tools you are given?

Think about how you can use that love to make things better around you.

How can you help others with that love?

Go where the love is.

> "The most important thing in the professional wrestling industry in this day and age of technology and the internet and social media is to be able to make wrestling unpredictable."
>
> — Matt Hardy

Matt Hardy wrestled his first WWF match in 1994, prior to his 21st birthday, far earlier than your average wrestler. Still active with WWE, Hardy has also had a longer career than most wrestlers. He is a 13-time world tag team champion, in addition to reigns as a TNA World Heavyweight Champion and an ECW championship. The smart money says he's a lock for the WWE Hall of Fame.

Hardy and his brother Jeff founded the OMEGA Championship Wrestling promotion as teenagers. Matt's work habits helped him accumulate an impressive track record. He has never been afraid to take risks, whether they were physical or creative.

Before YouTube channels became a mandatory outlet for public personas, Hardy launched *The Hardy Show* web series, then followed it with *The Matt Facts* and a *Final Deletion* story arc. Hardy instinctively grasped what so many creators in so many fields have learned: If you have undeniable metrics at your fingertips, your fans will support the company that supports you. With a measurable following, Hardy has always been able to find non-stop work with one major promotion or another, for two decades and counting.

In this internet era, "smart" fans feel like they have the inside track on storylines and hirings and firings — which are often intertwined. Surfing the web and gorging at the rumor mill, fans are still hungry for that increasingly rare commodity: a development they didn't see coming. When fans over-investigate the business or demand certain storylines, they love wrestling to death. Unpredictability is what keeps wrestling fresh and entertaining, whether it's a sudden swerve, unfortunate injury, unpredictable chemistry, or a spontaneous creative spark.

A routine will keep your life running smoothly. But unpredictable developments are what keep you coming back.

Think about the best moments of your life. Were they all planned out to the smallest detail? A few of them must have been spontaneous.

Sometimes you need to let life happen around you.

Don't let the internet and social media eat up your days. Especially your weekends.

Go out into the world.

See what happens.

Great things can happen when you are prepared, yet not planning every moment of every day. Leave time for the unpredictable. It will happen anyway.

Plan on it.

> **"Even if the character is something that seems ridiculous on paper, there's a human element to everything. Otherwise, we don't connect with it."**
>
> **— Cody Rhodes**

Cody Rhodes initially had bigger shoes to fill than most wrestlers. Ultimately, he decided to get his own shoes.

Cody is the son of the legendary Dusty Rhodes, The American Dream himself, one of the greatest to ever lace up boots and take the mic. Cody is the half-brother of the also-notable Goldust.

Wrestling recognized his pedigree and put it to work. Shortly after high school, he was signed to the WWE's developmental system. He made the company's main roster the following year, in 2007. Rhodes became a multi-time Intercontinental champion and Tag Team champion. And that impressive run in the biggest wrestling promotion pales compared to his career since he left it.

Following his departure, Rhodes promptly declared himself a free agent. Searching for his own identity, he wrestled among the ranks of Ring of Honor, TNA, New Japan Pro-Wrestling and a variety of top independent promotions. Rhodes become a main-eventer, a world champion and a major merchandise-mover — all this before co-producing the All In event with The Young Bucks. Rhodes not only remains a top-drawing talent on the global scene, but also serves as the executive vice president of All Elite Wrestling.

This quote dates back to when Cody was portraying the unsatisfying role of Stardust, who was essentially a face-painted comic book supervillain based on his brother's old character. Stardust's over-the-top image made crowds pop from time to time. The character was conceived to draw heat by hissing and throwing frequent in-ring tantrums. To Rhodes, it wasn't satisfying.

Rhodes wasn't enjoying his role, and it was contagious. He wasn't into Stardust, and neither were the fans. He wanted to develop a dramatic character, not play a cartoon.

Stardust looked ridiculous on paper.

The character lacked a human element.

The crowds didn't connect.

And neither did he.

Many very smart people with admirable tact find this fact distasteful, but it is a fact: Any time you engage in human interaction, you are selling yourself — or failing to sell yourself.

If you are always over-the-top, people will eventually tire of you. People want to see a human element in everyone and everything. Whether that means providing an unexpected laugh, shedding a tear or showing your human limitations through a loud cough that renders you momentarily helpless.

They want to connect with you.

Give them a connection.

> **"I don't play a character. It's totally just an extension of myself."**
>
> **— John Cena**

In 2019, John Cena is being billed by the WWE as "the greatest of all time." While it is difficult to identify "the greatest" anything in a scripted, collaborative form of entertainment, Cena has been working at the top of the WWE for over 15 years. He is not only a multi-time world champion, but looks poised to break Ric Flair's 16-time reign as world champion. And that count doesn't include Cena's multiple reigns with most of the WWE's other titles.

Cena has a reputation as the hardest-working man in the business because of his relentless schedule outside the ring. As a philanthropist, he has notably granted more wishes for the Make-A-Wish Foundation than any other celebrity, and was the first participant to grant 500. (Now he's closer to 600.) As an actor, he is a bona fide movie star, with A-list projects already announced through 2020. Working with WWE, he released a certified platinum album, 2014's *You Can't See Me*. And, as of this writing, the man is only 41 years old.

Cena has been working as a babyface for more of his career than not. His WWE character preaches the importance of "hustle, loyalty and respect." This overachieving — as paired with his inability to go on a long-term losing streak — has led many WWE fans to boo Cena, who has done everything possible to draw a universally positive reaction from the crowd.

Cena's P.M.A. and the hard-to-top work ethic radiate outside of the ring when he does press, reality television appearances and commercial endorsements. When he's outside the ring, he never seems far from his in-ring character. John Cena truly is John Cena.

When you're grappling with life, it helps if you can be yourself.

No one can maintain a false identity at all times. Even The Undertaker needs to show legal ID and answer questions for a TSA agent. People will see through a fake smile at some point, and they'll never welcome it the same way again.

If you are regularly portraying a persona other than your natural self, it is an act for other people. Sometimes you need to smile more than you want to. But don't let the facade override your personality.

Don't try to sell a false image. Focus on pushing the ball forward.

Don't worry about being a false recreation of somebody else's persona.

Be the best version of you that you can be — today.

And tomorrow, do a little better.

> "When you are superior like I am, it is hard to understand ignorance sometimes."

> — Roddy Piper

Rowdy Roddy Piper left this mortal coil years ago, but people still talk about him regularly. A true crossover icon, Piper starred in dozens of film and television projects, with roles ranging from the ass-kicking Nada in *They Live* to literary icon Oscar Wilde in *The Green Fairy*. He also found fresh acclaim in his later years as a podcaster and stand-up comic.

As a wrestler, Roddy Piper did not need to chase a title in order to be a main-eventer. He drew people in through his promos, which often felt like real, spontaneous dialogue from the meanest man alive. Any wrestler that has a recurring talk show-style segment owes a credit to Piper even today; *Miz TV* is clearly an homage to the groundbreaking *Piper's Pit* segment. Piper had such a storied career, the fact that he was in the main event of the first two WrestleManias is not even one of the first few things many people think of when Rowdy Roddy Piper comes to mind.

(His legend endured for years after his retirement, and his persona not only outlived his death, but became a transferable franchise. When Olympic medalist and UFC champion Ronda Rousey signed with the WWE, she adopted Piper's attitude, outfit, and name, wrestling as "Rowdy" Ronda Rousey.)

Even at his most popular, Piper was a heel crowds loved to hate. His confidence was undeniable and contagious. Piper refused to be ordinary or humble; in that regard, he was always a champion.

Piper was clearly deep in character when made that bold pronouncement. But that kind of statement — backed up by a flurry of fists and a willingness to bleed for our affection — made him a hardcore optimist. Piper believed in himself as much as anybody who walked the planet. And he delivered.

Calling yourself "superior" to others won't endear yourself to them; it worked for Piper, but he had something nobody else has. And your workplace probably won't be receptive to his shtick.

But…

If you don't believe in yourself, who will?

Speak up.

Take risks.

Make people notice you.

Defend yourself.

Will you settle for less? Is it OK if you don't achieve your full potential?

It wasn't OK for Rowdy Roddy Piper.

He did everything he could to achieve his personal goals. In his eyes, to do anything less was lazy, ignorant.

Are you satisfied with what you have?

To get what you want, are you willing to get rowdy?

> **"The joke we always say is that WWE doesn't pay us to wrestle — they pay us to travel."**
>
> **— Seth Rollins**

Seth Rollins has been recognized as top talent everywhere he worked. Prior to signing with the WWE, Rollins — then known as Tyler Black — was a world champion and tag champion for notable companies including Ring of Honor. At WWE, he is a multi-time World Heavyweight Champion, Tag Team Champion, Intercontinental Champion, and Grand Slam Champion.

Rollins' road was bumpy. Over his career, he demonstrated an amazing ability to rebound from injury. He has battled a variety of ailments and damage, yet he always manages to return to the ring better than ever.

His matches often involve flashy high-risk aerial maneuvers, yet Rollins also knows how to effectively tell a story in the ring. He is among the small group of current WWE talent that has headlined a WrestleMania.

Successful wrestlers famously spend more time on the road than home. WWE superstars not only face a physically grueling job; they do it while maintaining a heavy travel schedule. In an average week, Rollins appears on *Raw* and several house shows, in addition to whatever promotional appearances, pay-per-view events and WWE Network tapings are scheduled. Rollins is hinting that the actual wrestling is the fun part, while the travel is what feels like grueling work.

No matter the career you pursue — even if it is your dream job — some of it won't be interesting and fun.

Some of it will feel like a grind, whether it is travel, a rough commute, being on your feet all day, or being in the in-demand position you once fantasized about.

Sometimes, it helps to compartmentalize and remember why you are doing what you do. Even if your job feels like a grind, the work provides paychecks. And that income is enables you to pursue the goals, hobbies and passions of your choosing.

Take the good with the bad. Sometimes you just need to suck it up.

It's called *work* for a reason.

And they do give you money for it.

Sometimes that's good enough.

> **"The second you come through that curtain for a professional match, and all the fans start screaming and yelling and cheering, you feel it's worth all the bumps and bruises and sleepless nights."**
>
> **— Britt Baker**

Pennsylvania native Britt Baker has an advanced degree in kicking ass. She's always been a quick study.

Baker started wrestling on the indies in 2015. 2016 saw her first WWE match. Baker really stepped it up in 2018, with an NXT appearance against Shayna Baszler and a stand-out All In match alongside Tessa Blanchard, Madison Rayne and Chelsea Green. She had career options, more so than your average standout wrestler.

Instead of pursuing WWE stardom, she became a first-round signing for All Elite Wrestling, billed alongside Chris Jericho, PAC, MJF and SCU. And shortly before she signed to AEW, she became a certified medical doctor, graduating from the University Of Pittsburgh's School Of Dental Medicine.

Baker rose through the wrestling ranks while attending dental school. In a Pittsburgh *Post-Gazette* profile, writer Bill Schackner noted Baker had attended exams with "at least one black eye."

Sometimes, you have to endure some discomfort to get what you want.

If you want something extraordinary, prepare to pay an extraordinary cost.

You'll make it far in life if you can push through pain to achieve a goal.

To Baker, temporary suffering is worth a long-term gain.

They say nothing good comes easy. That sounds right.

Sometimes you have to literally fight for something you want.

Maybe you don't want to get off the couch and go to the gym. But if you do, you are edging closer to your fitness goal.

Maybe you don't want to go to the DMV. But if you do, you not only fulfill your legal obligations, you get that chore done and out of your life. You are, for a glorious but fleeting time, free.

If you're staring down a painful path, think about how good you'll feel once it's over.

Would you take a crushing blow to the face in exchange for making your dreams come true?

"WWE is like showbiz boot camp."

— Dean Ambrose

Dean Ambrose rose to the WWE from a pure professional-wrestling background. Unlike many of his WWE Superstar contemporaries, he was not a star athlete in college. In fact, he dropped out of high school to pursue his wrestling training.

While Ambrose may have been ring-ready before signing to WWE, physical skills aren't enough to make it as a pro.

To thrive it in the land of the McMahons, wrestlers need a variety of skills beyond the mat. When WWE develops talent, they school their prospective superstars in acting, public speaking and all sorts of communications-related skills. When a talent is called up to the main roster, they are expected to be well-rounded and able to perform in front of any audience on a moment's notice.

Ambrose is not exaggerating or bragging when he calls WWE a "showbiz boot camp." He has credits to back it up. Beyond WWE programming, he has appeared in several WWE-produced films, including *Countdown* and *12 Rounds 3: Lockdown*. As an actor, he usually nailed his lines on the first try. After years of wrestling, it was simple; live theater is a business where you don't get a second take.

You make progress as a professional — and as a person — by doing more, not less.

When you have a chance to attend training, workshops, seminars or other sorts of educational opportunities, you should take them, especially if they are offered through your company. When an employer is willing to invest in you, respect the effort. Show them what you can do. Employers want people who find a way to do more, not an excuse to do less.

Few of us will retire from the job we have in our 20s, 30s, or even 40s. A course or a seminar may provide skills you can take with you when you move on.

> "Wrestling is therapy. No matter how bad my personal situation is, when I step into the ring, all my troubles disappear. My baggage stays in the back, where it belongs."
>
> **— Eddie Guerrero**

During his 18-year career as a professional wrestler, Eddie Guerrero worked at a top level all over the world. One of the more successful members of the Guerrero wrestling dynasty, Eddie was a title-holder in WWE, WCW, ECW and AAA. Since his untimely passing in 2005, Guerrero has been inducted into the Halls Of Fame of the WWE, AAA and *Wrestling Observer Newsletter*. (WWE now owns, includes, and controls the legacies of the ECW and WCW.)

Guerrero was an effective and popular main-eventer as both a babyface and a heel. He regularly called out, "I lie! I cheat! I steal!" He would do anything needed in order to win a match. And the crowds still loved him.

Guerrero could do all of the fast-paced Lucha-style work in the ring. And he could also work against bigger competitors in a slower, strong-style approach. No matter the competitor, Guerrero indisputably could get a great match out of them.

Much like a musician views songwriting as a craft, the majority of wrestlers see wrestling as their chosen art form. They view their matches as a means of expressing themselves. Performers often say they're happiest when performing for a crowd.

Wrestlers are no different. It is the time when they have to focus on entertaining spectators. For a handful of moments, all their problems are turned down or disappear, from troubles at home to nagging injuries. They send their best energy out to an appreciative crowd, where it multiplies and returns in waves. Flooded with adrenaline and love, wrestlers bask in the spotlight. With every cheer and boo, the audience plays a meaningful role in the event. It's a kind of communion few people ever feel.

Work can be therapy.

Work can be meaningful.

Work is a chance to make something happen. Maybe something unique. Maybe you can create something that will outlive you. Maybe something unique and special that will dissipate like smoke, then live only in memories.

We perform best when we focus like Guerrero. We stop focusing on all the things that might go wrong. We put our heads down and do what we need to do. We forget our phones and our problems and our bills.

When he was in the ring, Guerrero lived in the moment. And he learned to enjoy it while it lasted — which we often forget to do.

When you truly focus on work, all you have is the moment.

And while it lasts, that moment is enough.

> **"Being a wrestler is like walking on the treadmill of life. You get off it and it just keeps going."**
>
> **— Randy Savage**

Wrestling has an appeal like nothing else. No wonder most grapplers won't let it go. As he did with most aspects of the business, the mighty Randy Savage handled his exit in a unique fashion. Aside from some work with TNA in late 2004 and early 2005, Savage mostly avoided the wrestling business after leaving WCW. He shifted his focus to film and television projects. He even recorded a hip-hop album titled *Be a Man*.

Savage's distinguished late-career WCW run came because Vince McMahon believed Savage was already too old to be wrestling. He was wrong.

Savage commanded crowds and respect in the WCW, where he had a few more world title runs from 1994 through 2000. As he entered his twilight, Savage gave back to the business. He had a reputation elevating the careers of other wrestlers, which he did for Diamond Dallas Page, a series of female valets, and a variety of NWO stable members. When he signed with the WCW, he also made sure that his brother Lanny had a job in the promotion.

Unlike many of his contemporaries, Savage stopped wrestling before his career bottomed out. Whether they do it for love, fun or money, some competitors from the first few WrestleMania cards still wrestle on the independent circuit. Not a lot of footage is publicly available from the last few years of Savage's life. The public image of the buff Macho Man is never far from his peak.

Savage finds resonant wisdom in one of the wrestler's indispensable working tools, that all-weather cardio machine, the treadmill.

Wrestlers have an uncommon grasp of mortality. Some stare it down. Some run from it.

As a wrestler, you need the treadmill. But the treadmill doesn't need you.

Some wrestlers only accept that inescapable truth in their last agonizing steps.

Savage didn't need a reminder.

No matter how great you are or were, your business is going to keep going, with a new set of faces. You may live long enough to retire and call it a day. But everyone else still has to make a living.

Think about the future.

Do you want future generations to have it even better than you do?

You can't take it with you when your time is up.

What are you doing now to make your business — your world — a better place?

If you share your experience with others, your name and knowledge and skills might live on. Pass them along to another person who can use them.

Leave the business better than you found it. Elevate the game.

And if you do things right, people will still be talking about you favorably — as they do Randy Savage — long after you have passed on.

1. Develop and pursue ambitions

Successful wrestlers have goals. And when they reach them, they set new ones. They don't want to repeat what they did yesterday. They want to accomplish more. If you accomplish more, you are likely to get more.

2. Develop, demonstrate and broadcast character

When you think of a good wrestler, you have an idea who they are. So who are you? What do you represent? What kind of thing do you do? Are they good things? If so, people will want you around.

3. Ponder psychology

Workers who are in demand consider how people will react to what they do. And they anticipate how their actions will make people feel.

4. Talk good and interestingly

Popular wrestlers practice verbal communication, then execute it well. They convey character, explain agendas, and generate interest. Maybe they phrase things in a colorful fashion to get your attention. (See what we did there?)

5. Put on a show

Sadly, exceptional ability and quality content can be subtle distinctions — important ones, no doubt. But mere quality doesn't always attract the eye and ear. When preparing any kind of presentation, ask yourself: What can you do to make it *not boring*?

6. Prepare

Ambitious and effective people don't just wait for opportunities; they prepare for them. And when an opportunity presents itself, a pro is ready to go.

7. Take bumps

Wrestlers pay a price every time they step in a ring. They do the hard parts. Ever business is full of people who want the paycheck, glory, and status. There's a much shorter list of people who will do the work.

8. Exercise

Exercise keeps you going strong. It helps you feel good when the times are tough. It engages the body so the mind can drift and connect new ideas. Take care of your machine. And it will take care of you.

9. Do what is right for the business

Successful wrestlers do what is right for the institution, even if it means limiting their personal glory at the moment. A true professional is not afraid to drop a belt, end a streak, or make an inferior partner look good. You can advance your own interests by adding value and serving others.

10. Think about it — and think big

Successful professionals study their business. What do successful people do? What has been done before? What has *not* been done before? What can you do that other people won't? What can you do that other people can't? What can you — and only you — do? Find that out, and you will possess a unique value. And, in the right showcase, you are now uniquely valuable. So go find your arena.

Emma (left) and Britt Baker. By Ed Battes.

Darren's 10 Favorite Wrestlers of All Time

... and Why

In every way possible, professional wrestling is full of subjectivity. What I look for in a five-star match could be the exact opposite of what you want to see. Furthermore, you may be cheering for a wrestler for the very same reason I am rolling my eyes.

Thanks to a very patient father, I did get to see many of the all-time greats — to name a few, Andre The Giant, Hulk Hogan, Roddy Piper, Ric Flair, Sting, The Undertaker, Jimmy Snuka — wrestle in-person when I was a kid. But I am more partial to the wrestling of the last 20 years, given that this time period has included the peak of WCW and ECW, the ascent of Ring of Honor, the internationalization of New Japan, and the regrowth of independent and territorial wrestling.

It's an exciting time to be a fan, with more wrestling than ever to enjoy, no matter what your preference.

Following is a list of my 10 favorite wrestlers of all-time, not in any order. They're all great in their own way. That's why they're great. There's nobody else like them.

— DP

1. Chris Jericho

We Jericholics have numerous reasons for our Jericholicism. But I'll zone in on one: Chris Jericho's persistence has made him the David Bowie of professional wrestling.

Bowie regularly changed up his character from album to album — creating new characters including Ziggy Stardust, The Thin White Duke and Aladdin Sane. Over the years, Jericho has reinvented himself as Y2J, Lion Heart, Ayatollah Of Rock N Rolla and the Best In The World, among others, past and, no doubt, the future.

Jericho has also changed up his in-ring style regularly over the years. He is able to blend together Lucha, Japanese strong style and fast-paced cruiserweight moves with the WWE's more entertainment-based form of wrestling. It all adds up in a performer who has been unpredictable for decades. Jericho's recent signing with All Elite Wrestling continues the narrative of him always charting new territory.

2. The Young Bucks

I have had the pleasure of seeing The Young Bucks work in all sorts of settings and configurations over the past five years. And by that I don't just mean that I saw them wrestle on a cruise ship. I have watched them wrestle as both babyfaces and heels, and in both standard tag and six-man matches. No matter where the match was and who else was involved, it was full of action, and it still told a gripping a story.

In-ring craft aside, The Young Bucks also apply an admirable DIY work ethic. While The Bucks are not synonymous with punk rock from a visual or aural perspective, there was something fierce, raw and minimal in the way they defied the tried and true blueprints for how a wrestler "should" look and act. Their career is absolutely punk-minded. They created their own scene of like-minded individuals, much like how Gilman Street in the California's Bay Area was a home to Green Day, Operation Ivy (the precursor to Rancid) and a lot of West Coast punk rock's originals.

Ultimately, The Young Bucks have the potential to go down as the best tag team of all-time, as suggested by everything from memorable matches to merch sales. A tag team's success is often judged in what happens after that team disbands — whether they split and stage a long-term feud, or they become shining new singles stars. Yet The Bucks are the rare tag team the majority of fans don't want to see break up anytime soon — if ever.

3. Daniel Bryan

I didn't watch much wrestling between 1994 and 2008; music entirely consumed me when I was a teenager. In 2009 I was dragged to a Ring of Honor show at New York's Hammerstein Ballroom. The bill included the pre-WWE likes of Kevin Owens, Sami Zayn, Seth Rollins, Cesaro, Daniel Bryan and Austin Aries. That was the first time I would see a match by Daniel Bryan — then working as Bryan Danielson. It was a revelation. I was blown away when I realized the true artistry he applies towards his wrestling.

Whether you became a fan of him as Daniel Bryan or Bryan Danielson, his matches have always been great. He can tell a great story no matter whether he is portraying the babyface or the heel. Size-wise, he is smaller than the majority of competitors he faces. But you can tell he hits hard. And he is able to show you he is as strong as men who are bigger than him. He is believable.

D-Bry's current WWE run as a heel is refreshing, since he is getting to flex one of his key strengths: delivering heat-seeking promos. He is so well-regarded that audiences struggle to boo him. So undoubtedly if/when Daniel Bryan turns babyface again, he will be received so favorably that the WWE may have to rethink the company line about John Cena being "the greatest of all time."

4. Mr. Perfect

Mr. Perfect was one of my favorites when I was in elementary school, and I'm not sure why that is. I wasn't super into heels. It may have had something to do with him being in the WWF Wrestlefest arcade game, which I definitely pumped hundreds of dollars of quarters into over the years.

Upon further thought, it may have had something to do with Mr. Perfect's finishing move, the Perfectplex, looking cool. It may have had something to do with the vignettes that established his character's superhuman perfection, like the one where he threw a Hail Mary touchdown pass — to himself.

Whatever it was, Curt Hennig was undoubtedly one of the all-time greats.

5. Vader

Vader is widely regarded as one of the best "big men" to ever participate in professional wrestling. I see him as one of the best ever, period. He could do a lot of the moves that a cruiserweight or luchador could do, even though he clocked in over 400 pounds.

Vader was believable as a monster heel, and unstoppable. His career ran around 30 years. He wrestled with all of the big companies at some point. He also managed to take his wrestling name with him wherever he went, doing so in eras when other competitors were not able to do that. Simply put, you are missed, Vader.

6. Jushin "Thunder" Liger

As of this writing, Jushin "Thunder" Liger is still an active in-ring competitor. I had the pleasure of seeing him wrestle in person in the early 1990s against Brian Pillman at a WCW house show in New Jersey. I can't tell you what the outcome of the match was, or if it was comparable to their *Clash Of The Champions* match. But I remember non-stop excitement.

Two decades later, I caught Liger at a Ring of Honor event — I believe it was in a match against Adam Cole — and at a big NXT show against Tyler Breeze. Liger is one of the few masked performers who can truly tell a story without facial expressions. He was still performing at a high level when many of his peers were relegated to only doing tag matches with minimal bumps.

Without Jushin "Thunder" Liger's influence, I'm not sure if WCW or WWE would have ever done so much with cruiserweights. And it's pretty amazing when you think about it: Liger managed to accomplish so much of his career in English-speaking countries without promos or merchandising. He got himself over for decades, entirely based on in-ring ability.

7. Ricky "The Dragon" Steamboat

Many people regard Ricky "The Dragon" Steamboat as half of one of the greatest matches of all-time: his *WrestleMania 3* bout with Randy "Macho Man" Savage. But Steamboat was part of so many great feuds that it's almost disrespectful to say he definitively hit his peak with that 1987 match. After all, that DDT "on the concrete" spot with Jake Roberts is still talked about, as are his hour-long matches with Ric Flair. His feud with Chris Jericho in the 2000s was also very impressive: Steamboat in his 50s could still outwork most of the WWE roster.

When it comes to his in-ring matches, Steamboat was one of the few performers who did not need a gimmick to shine. When you think about it, his "The Dragon" era in WWF had him working on the lower-card, while his "Family Man" character for WCW also kept him away from the main-event pitch. In other words, the guy was — to reference an old-timer cliché — no sizzle and all steak. Steamboat's arm-drag is probably the coolest-looking arm-drag in wrestling, past or present.

To top it all off, I had the pleasure of meeting him on Chris Jericho's wrestling cruise. He could not have been more gracious. He stayed around 90 minutes longer than contracted, made meaningful conversation with everyone in line, and still spoke to everyone who approached him during the rest of the cruise. Talented, pleasant and gracious — not something that you can say about every wrestler you meet, eh?

8. A.J. Styles

Admittedly, I am very late to the A.J. Styles bandwagon. I didn't watch TNA or Impact when he was part of the company. As I had with Daniel Bryan, I went to a Ring of Honor event, heard everyone going crazy for him, and then sort of got it. His match was not all high spots, unlike others on that event. Nor was it all technical. But he managed to find a way to tell a story while still selling a character and creating exciting moments.

Since his debut in WWE over three years ago, Styles has made it clear that he is one of the best wrestlers on the roster. It is nearly-impossible to have a bad match when Styles is in the mix. He excels as both a babyface and a heel, having filled both roles while holding WWE's top title. He also helped prove that a main-roster WWE talent does not have to go through NXT or change their name before signing to WWE.

At age 41, A.J. Styles is still one of the best wrestlers in the world. If he stays healthy and injury-free, he will continue to redefine what wrestlers can accomplish in their 40s.

9. Randy "Macho Man" Savage

Savage was legendary for requiring serious scripting in all his matches, since he took wrestling very seriously as his craft. He did not "call it in the ring" like many of his peers. He wanted to make sure that every move mattered.

Great matches aside, Savage portrayed an original persona unlike any other, simultaneously flamboyant and tough. He regularly changed his look, keeping things current, definitely more so than a lot of his peers. He was arguably the first major wrestler to regularly evolve with the times. Many of the legends — Hulk Hogan and Ric Flair included— would not change characters or looks until after things had grown stale. And thankfully that rolling-with-the-times gave us the *Be A Man* rap album.

Savage was also a bigger part of mainstream popular culture than almost any other wrestler that you can think of. People are still talk about him, quote him, and imitate him all the time. Thankfully his brother, "The Genius" Lanny Poffo, is helping to keep Savage's legacy alive, as is the WWE Network.

10. Diamond Dallas Page

To be clear, I was not much of a wrestling fan throughout most of Diamond Dallas Page's career as a full-time in-ring performer. But in catching up on his legacy through the WWE Network, reading his books, listening to his appearances on podcasts, watching *The Resurrection of Jake the Snake* and so forth, I see someone who was way ahead of their time.

A lot of the things DDP did were not "cool" at the time, but if you look back at them with your 2019 glasses on, you see that they stand the test of time pretty well.

Most importantly, DDP is helping wrestlers— both past and present, including some on this list— stay healthy, thanks to DDP Yoga. So he deserves to be on just about any Top 10 list related to wrestlers who have done well for themselves.

Ferris' 10 Favorite Wrestlers of All Time

(Who Darren Didn't

Pick Already, Mostly)

[In Alphabetical Order]

Andre the Giant

Growing up in the 1970s and 80s, you heard semi-plausible suburban legends, mostly via *In Search Of...* and *The Guinness Book of World Records*: Kids talked about UFOs. An unearthed Noah's Ark. Spontaneous human combustion. Bigfoot. An undefeated wrestler who was 7 feet tall and weighed 500 pounds. Most of them were a bust. Not Andre the Giant.

As director Jason Hehir's excellent *Andre the Giant* documentary deftly observes, Andre was a borderline supernatural figure who could attract your attention to pro wrestling and keep it there. After a brief star turn in the Hollywood classic *The Princess Bride*, the beloved legend died at the age of 46, having proven he was as good—and big—as it gets.

Kurt Angle

Full disclosure: I'm a Pittsburgh guy. Pittsburgh is widely known as The City of Champions. And Kurt Angle and Bruno Sammartino are the two most highly decorated professional wrestlers. So they're *objectively* as distinguished as the Steel Curtain Steelers and the *Fam-il-ee* Pirates. Kurt Angle won an Olympic gold medal in wrestling, *with a broken neck.*

As a pro wrestler, Angle made it big as an oblivious jackass, a comedic character like Daffy Duck. But his indisputable record made him a credible role model with *useful* slogans, like his famous Three I's: Intensity, Integrity, and Intelligence. *That's* how you get over. It's true. It's true.

Chyna

As of this writing, Chyna has been announced as a WWE Hall of Fame Inductee, as part of the game-changing stable D-Generation X. If life is fair, she will enter the Hall with her own spot. But as the life and career of the late, great wrestler — born Joan Laurer — show, life is not fair.

Year after year, Chyna went toe-to-toe with male heavyweight greats. Chiseled and ominous, she entered the spotlight as the bodyguard to DX stars Shawn Michaels and HHH. On her own, she was the first and only woman wrestler to hold the Intercontinetal Belt. She set the bar for what a girl can do in the business. And she remains a respected trailblazer.

Diamond Dallas Page

Full disclosure II: DDP kindly wrote the foreword to this book, but he was already on our lists. DDP never gave up on his dreams. He entered wrestling late in life. He became the oldest wrestler to win a world championship, taking the WCW strap at a time when wrestling was dense with star-powered talent, and the business was the hottest it ever had been.

But for my money, his life after wrestling is what makes him a true champion and leader. Years of in-ring damage led him to develop the healing exercise practice DDP Yoga, which is changing millions of lives, mine included. DDP is a force for good.

Mick Foley

Mick Foley never looked like a first-round draft pick, but he always performed like an MVP. But he knew what he wanted. And he became one of the greats, a three-time WWF champion who bled his way to the top.

In the 1980s, cage matches were a thing of legend — and rightly so. But pre-Attitude Era cages were modest 8-foot chain link fences. Foley made reality eclipse the legend. His most famous match is the seminal 1998 Hell in a Cell match, in which the Undertaker threw him *off the roof* of a 16-foot cage. Defeated but not broken, Foley became a star with wattage to match The Rock at his peak.

The hardcore legend later proved he has smarts to match, as a stand-up comic, storyteller, and author of two New York *Times* no. 1 bestsellers.

Lita

The Rock and Wrestling Connection comes and goes, with mixed results. After decades of experimentation, wrestling finally got it right by letting Lita be herself. She's as cool as any wrestler who ever laced up the boots.

Tattooed, pierced, and flying high, Lita helped keep the Attitude wave rolling into the 21st century. Fearless, she studied in Mexico, graduated to ECW, and became an equally valuable part of the high-flying Hardy Boyz' Team Xtreme. After a stint fronting rock band the Luchagors, the four-time champion returned to the ring and eventually soared into the WWE Hall of Fame. And she made it because she was authentic.

Rowdy Roddy Piper

Rowdy Roddy Piper's string of indellible performances include a largely forgotten segment that was an all-time-great moment for fans who followed the larger continuum of wrestling itself.

Greg "The Hammer" Valentine had — according to legend — permanently *mutilated* Piper during their NWA feud. A year later, Piper had resettled in the WWF, as the firebrand host of the talk show-within-a-show, *Piper's Pit*. Then one night, Valentine walked onto Piper's set. Harsh words were exchanged. As a young mark, I was absolutely certain one of them was going to murder the other, live on TV.

Then things took a sudden turn. And I couldn't believe it. Because Piper—a celebrated Hollywood actor, popular comic and enthralling podcaster—was one of the greatest storytellers to ever grace the ring.

The Road Warriors

I've blown money, bashed my skull, and damaged my hearing in the pursuit of the fastest, hardest, toughest music I could find. The Road Warriors are as *metal* as anything I've ever witnessed.

Watching Hawk and Animal destroy all competition in tiny NWA studio rings was like seeing the mighty Metallica play club shows. Carved from granite and painted like demons, they were lords of the wasteland, utterly believable in every second of their unstoppable in-ring domination.

Bruno Sammartino

Bruno Sammartino wore the belt longer than anybody else. He was huge in every possible way, even by modern standards. *Look* at the guy. Without steroids, he was a monster, impossibly thick. But he was a beloved behemoth, a man of respect.

Mr. Sammartino was a man of principle. In the 1960s, he spent political capital unsuccessfully trying to unionize the business. Still, he personally carried wrestling to unprecedented heights — see page 57 for a rundown of some amazing career stats.

When wrestling went supernova in the 1980s, he quietly worked his way out of the spotlight, refusing to debase his reality-based character for more paydays. Because he had *enough*. He was model of integrity, loyalty and moderation. We will never see his equal.

Kairi Sane

Knowing full-well how the business works, I watch international star Kairi Sane — the Pirate Princess of NXT — and I still can't believe my eyes.

Every off-the-top-rope InSane elbow drop is clearly, *clearly* a life-threatening maneuver that permanently damages both parties... right?

With a trained eye, I *still* mark the hell out. My thoughts are hijacked by an over-the-top announcer: "OH MY GOD! KAIRI SANE HAS LITERALLY DECIMATED HER! SHE'LL NEVER BE THE SAME!"

Because she is that damned good.

All websites accessed November 2018-February 2019.

QUOTES:

Ric Flair: Many times and places. Witness it in "To Be The Man" on YouTube. com, posted 30 July 2007, by user krayven76.

Big E: Neil Docking's "WWE Superstar Big E..." Mirror Online. 20 Feb. 2016. Mirror.co.uk.

AJ Lee: "WrestleMania Diary: AJ Lee, Day 2." 4 April 2013. WWE.com.

Triple H: Twitter tweet by HHH. 5 February 2019. Twitter.com/TripleH.

DDP on 90%: Page, D. "DDP's Living Life at 90%..." 2014. At Vimeo.com.

Larry Zbyszko: From Twitter account Wrestling Quotes, @JustRasslin. Quoted 22 Sep 2018.

Dwayne "The Rock" Johnson: From Instagram account Creating Success. Posted 3 April 2018. Instagram.com/success.creating.

Scott Hall: From 2014 WWE Hall of Fame induction speech. "2014 WWE Hall of Fame Inductee: Razor Ramon: Raw, March 24, 2014." At WWE YouTube channel. Posted 24 March 2014.

Lita: From Lita WWF bio, archived at fan site Hardy Boyz and Lita, Tripod.com.

DDP on haters: S.R. Sapp's "DDP Speaks About Helping Bring Scott Hall And Kevin Nash Into WCW..." 29 May 2016. For WrestlingInc.com.

Eric Bischoff: From Bischoff & Jeremy Roberts' Controversy Creates Cash. 2006. New York: Pocket Books.

Edge: Adam Copeland. Adam Copeland On Edge. Original edition 2004, World Wrestling Entertainment Books. From paperback edition, 2005, Gallery Books.

Randy Orton: B. Campbell's "Randy Orton Reflects on his Royal Rumble win." 3 February 2017. ESPN.com. Is anyone reading this? Tweet us if you see it.

Ultimate Warrior: From WWE Hall of Fame Induction speech. "2014 WWE Hall of Famer Ultimate Warrior speaks: Raw, April 7, 2014." WWE YouTube channel.

Vince McMahon: Kevin Cook's "Playboy Interview: Vince McMahon." Playboy February 2001, pp. 55-68.

Lawler: From Twitter account Wrestling Quotes, @JustRasslin. Quoted 12 Oct 2018.

Shawn Michaels: Popular HBK T-shirt.

Bruno Sammartino: Sammartino, Bob Michelucci, Paul McCollough. Bruno Sammartino: An Autobiography of Wrestling's Living Legend. 2008. Createspace.

Dave "Batista" Bautista: T. Gilchrist's "SDCC: Marvel's "Guardians" Expand the Studio's Cinematic Galaxy." 5 August 2013. From CBR.com.

Paul Heyman: M. Hines' "WWE and ECW Legend Paul Heyman: The Malcolm McLaren of Professional Wrestling." 1 August 2014. At Independent.co.uk.

Mark Henry: D. Paltrowitz's "WWE Hall of Famer Mark Henry on his early days with The Rock, scouting talent for WWE & more." 8 November 2018. At TheHypeMagazine.com.

Salina de la Renta: D. Paltrowitz's "MLW Star Salina De La Renta On Her First Acting Role, Career Goals & Last Words For The Kids."13 January 2018, from TheHypeMagazine.com.

Billy Corgan: M. Hester's "Smashing Pumpkins' Billy Corgan Talks His Passion for Pro Wrestling!" 26 September 2017. From BleacherReport.com.

Andy Kaufman: D. Hirshey's "Andy Kaufman Was One Truly Wild and Truly Crazy Man." 15 May 2016. From TheDailyBeast.com.

CM Punk: J. Robinson's "CM Punk Talks Rock, Austin, 'WWE 12'." 23 November 2011. From ESPN.com.

Roman Reigns: J. Caudill's "Roman Reigns Talks 'Royal Rumble,' Injury Return & Haters." 2290 January 2015. From CraveOnline.com.

Jesse Ventura: V.Z. Mercogliano's "Meet the Champs..." 14 February 2017. From Lohud.com.

Gail Kim: J. Barnett. "Gail Kim Talks Hall of Fame Induction..." 29 September 2016. From USAtoday.com.

Chris Jericho: R. McNicol's "Chris Lifts Lid on Punk Performances." 05 Apri 2016. From TheSun.co.uk.

DDP on reality programs: J. Stewart's. "Punk, Jericho Fight Over Belt." 31 March 2012. At Newsday.com.

Dean Ambrose: Twitter fan account @AmbroseQuotes, archived 23 Aug 2014.

Mick Foley: Legendary quote widely attributed to Foley.

Ric Flar, preternatural genius: WWE's "The 100 Best Matches to See Before You Die. 24 Feb 2017. WWE.com.

Young Bucks: M. Jackson & M. Jackson's "The Young Bucks on Why Working for WWE Isn't Important to Them." 15 November 2017. From PWpodcasts.com.

Daniel Bryan: D. Bryan & C. Tello's Yes!: My Improbable Journey to the Main Event of WrestleMania. 2016. London: Ebury Press.

Matt Hardy: "Exclusive Interview With Matt Hardy." 11 Mar 2017. ROHwrestling.com.

Cody Rhodes: C. Radish's "'Arrow' Season 5: Cody Rhodes on Playing Oliver's New Adversary..." 19 October 2016. From Collider. com.

John Cena: J. Robinson's. "WrestleMania 29: John Cena talks The Rock." 05 April 2013. From ESPN.com.

Roddy Piper: Quote archived at Twitter fan account @JustRasslin. 2 November 2018.

Seth Rollins: C. Crowder's "WWE Champ Seth Rollins on Life as Pro Wrestler..." Des Moines Register. 6 May 2015. At DesMoinesRegister.com.

Britt Baker: B. Schnackner's "By day Britt Baker Is a Dental Student..." 18 October 2017. Pittsburgh Post-Gazette. At Post-Gazette.com.

Dean Ambrose on preparation: B. Fritz. "WWE's Dean Ambrose Brings the Action to Big Screen..." 19 August 2017. From SportingNews.com/

Eddie Guerrero: E. Guerrero & M. Krugman. Cheating Death, Stealing Life: The Eddie Guerrero Story. 2006. Gallery Books.

Randy Savage: M. Mooneyham's "'Macho Man' Was a True Original.21 May 2011. From PostAndCourier.com.

OTHER SOURCES CITED:

Rogan: The Joe Rogan Experience: "#1254: Dr. Phil." 26 Feb. 2019. At JoeRogan.net.

Oswalt: Off Camera With Sam Jones: "Patton Oswalt." 4 March 2019.

Baslione: Terribly Funny with Steve Basilone podcast: "Matt Bush." 27 Feb 2019.

1: Marisa Guthrie's "How Fox Bodyslammed Rivals to Win WWE Rights." 30 May 2018. Hollywood Reporter online, at HollywoodReporter.com.

2: "WWE Reports Record Revenue and Strong Q2 2018 Results." Press release from WWE. 26 July 2018. At Corporate.WWE.com.

3: Vince Lombardi, as quoted in Vince Lombardi Jr.'s book, What It Takes to Be #1: Vince Lombardo on Leadership. 2003. NY: McGraw-Hill Education.

4: "Highest Grossing Stars of 2018 at the Domestic Box Office." The Numbers. At www.The-Numbers.com. Accessed January 2019.

5: Natalie Robehmed's "Chris Hemsworth Is The Top-Grossing Actor Of 2018." 31 December 2018. Forbes online. At Forbes.com.

6: John Lynch's "The 50 Actors Who Have Made the Most Money at the US Box Office." Business Insider. 2 September 2018. At BusinessInsider.com.

7: Pat Conroy's My Losing Season. Page 400. 2002. NY: Nan A. Talese/Doubleday.

8: "Nine Things You Need to Know About Bruno Sammartino." WWE Staff. 18 April 2018. For WWE.com.

9: Bruno Sammartino, Bob Michelucci, and Paul McCollough's Bruno Samamartino: An Autobiography of Wrestling's Living Legend. 2008. Createspace.

10: Mike Mooneyham's "An Incredible Life: Bruno Sammartino Was the Real People's Champion." 28 April 2018. The Post and Courier. PostAndCourier.com.

11: Jon Robinson's "WWE to Induct Bruno Sammartino into HOF." 04 February 2013. ESPN.com.

12: McMahon tweet. 18 Apr 2018. "One of the finest..." Twitter.com/VinceMcMahon.

INDEX

Thanks — first and foremost — to **Melissa** for the daily support (and feedback); this project could not and would not have happened without you.

Mom & Dad, by example, you instilled it in me that it was possible to be a published writer. (**Adam & Shari**, you two finely exemplify that Paltrowitz-style creativity on a regular basis, as do **Blair & Mike**.)

Further love, thanks, apologies and / or gratitude goes out to the **Andreev, Milman, Cohen, Arbakow, Chavez-Young, Balsirow, Goldberg, Diaz, Segal, Mones, Fink, and Post families** for their ongoing assistance.

Diamond Dallas Page, thanks for the excellent foreword, beyond the positively unstoppable encouragement from both you and Brenda.

Maria Ferrero, you probably have no idea of the role you played in making this book happen — and that's actually really funny.

And last but not least, **D.X. Ferris**, you're one of the few people that not only practices what they preach but actually gets stuff done. Thanks for that, and hope to do another one of these sorts of books with you again in the near future.

Positive Darren Paltrowitz. The walk was walked, brutha!

Diamond Dallas Page, Brenda, Rob, Steve, Lexy, Rachel, and everybody on the DDP team, past & present.

Hardcore Nicholas Higgins and **Ed "Badass" Battes**. You're both heavyweight champ-eens.

Brendan "Bruiser" Halpin and **Jason "Nuke" Novak**, the scientific babyfaces of the copy-editing community.

Jumpin' Jayson Shenk, for expert photo retouching.

The Wolfpack: Maria Ferrero, Arp Laszlo, Scott Whitt, NoFriender, Dragon King Karl, Justin Pierott, and **Matt "The Amish Sheik" Neff**.

Tony Erba, the Parma Puncher, who will blade if he has to.

Everybody at 11AM: Andy, Mark, Mike, Steve & CEO Joe.

All the photographers and behind-the-scenes people who lined us up with this, that, the other thing, and the other guy.

Alan "Maddog" Natali, the other Italian Strongman.

Bill "Powerhouse" Hughes, the wrestling king of the Mon Valley, the Paul Heyman of the CWF. Guys like Powerhouse keep it alive on a local level.

Alex, Eric & Mandy for true highlights of the Attitude Era.

R.I.P.:

Ronald Forythe, Andre the Giant, King Kong Bundy, Chyna, Chris Bryan/Chandler Biggins, and **Bruno Sammartino**. Also **The Pittsburgh Civic Arena**. And my late, great dad, **Sumner J. Ferris**, who took us to Hulkamania-era WWF shows and loathed every minute. But he sucked it up, because that's what good parents do.

(Dad also interceded and saved my younger brother **James** from many a figure-four leglock and Cobra Clutch. I should have known better. Sorry, J. Don't let Sumner and Max take it too far.)

This book was co-written to instrumental Nine Inch Nails and Trent Reznor-Atticus Ross tracks.

Everybody at home: Love is like a rock.

Darren Paltrowitz

Darren Paltrowitz is a New York resident with over 15 years of entertainment industry experience.

He began working around the music business as a teenager, interning for the manager of his then-favorite band Superdrag.

In the years following, he has worked with a wide array of artists including OK Go, They Might Be Giants, Mike Viola, Tracy Bonham, Loudness, Rachael Yamagata, and Amanda Palmer.

Darren's writing has appeared in dozens of outlets including the *New York Daily News*, Inquisitr, Urbanmatter, The Daily Meal, The Hype Magazine, *All Music Guide*, *Guitar World*, TheStreet.com, *Format Magazine*, *Businessweek*, *The Improper*, the L.A. *Times*, and *The Jewish Journal*.

Darren is also the host of *The Paltrocast With Darren Paltrowitz* podcast, which is co-produced with PureGrainAudio.

He is the author of the book *Pocket Change: Your Happy Money*.

He is a proud resident of Long Beach, New York with his wife Melissa.

Follow him online:

Facebook.com/DarrenPaltrowitz

Twitter.com/Paltrowitz

Instagram.com/Paltrowitz

Paltrowitz.com

D.X. Ferris

D.X. Ferris is a communication coach, consultant, and professor. He has won numerous writing awards, including the Ohio Society of Professional Journalists' Best Reporter of the Year.

For 20 years, Ferris has written for newspapers and magazines, including America's top two music publications: *Alternative Press* and *Rolling Stone*.

His previous motivational and how-to books document best practices in martial arts, parenting, and non-profit leadership.

His rock books include the official biography of Donnie Iris & the Cruisers. He wrote two volumes about heavy metal heroes Slayer, one of which is part of Bloomsbury's *33 1/3* series, the vanguard collection in music writing. He...

...ghostwrites and produces.

...has practiced his craft over 10,000 hours.

...has graded over 5,000 speeches.

...is a third-degree black belt in Taekwondo.

...designed and produced the CWF print program.

...is a husband and father of two.

...lost 40 pounds and rebooted his flagging health over a year, with the DDP Yoga fitness program.

...picked up the nickname ten years before D-Generation X was a thing. But don't get him wrong; he has plenty of DX shirts.

His *Goodfellas* book is his TED Talk.

Follow him at Twitter.com/DXFerris.

DXFerris.com

For Whom the Cowbell Tolls:
25 Years of Paul's Boutique

by Peter Relic and Dan LeRoy,
author of *33 1/3: Beastie Boys' Paul's Boutique*

Think you know everything possible about the Beastie Boys classic album Paul's Boutique? Think again. To commemorate the album's 25th birthday, author Dan LeRoy and journalist Peter Relic joined forces to "drop the new science and kick the new knowledge" about this legendary 1989 release. This all-new book is crammed with deep research and fresh information. These cats found legit diamonds that even the *Beasties* didn't know about.

"If you are a music fan, Dan LeRoy's obsessive work covering the Beastie Boys' most fascinating and complicated album, *Paul's Boutique*, is essential reading."
— **Brian Coleman**, author of *Check the Techniaue* and *Rakim Told Me*

POCKET CASH

YOUR *HAPPY* MONEY

DARREN PALTROWITZ
Dr. JERI FINK & DONNA PALTROWITZ

Slayer Books & News
@SlayerBook

Following ⌄

pssst
new-look expanded edition of slayer
book
paperback
6 new chapters
24 new pages
is a mere
$16.66
$6.66 ebook
at amazon
slayerbio.com
new look is...

SLAYER BIOGRAPHY

SLAYER 66 2/3: THE JEFF & DAVE YEARS...

POST-REPENTLESS REMASTERED EDITION

BY D.X. FERRIS

6623 PRESS
MOTIVATIONAL

• AKRON •

Version 1.0: April 7, 2019

6623 Press: Useful, creator-owned, unconventional, reasonably priced books about popular culture, success and other cool stuff.

www.6623Press.com

6623 Press can bring speakers who are not boring to your live event. For information about special discounts for bulk purchases, contact 6623 Press: 6623Press@gmail.com / 6623Press.com

Cover Illustration & Layout by **Nick Higgins Design**
© 2019 Nick Higgins

Proofreaders: Brendan Halpin, Jason Novak

Photos ©, by, and courtesy of...
DDP courtesy DDP Yoga. **Cody & Delirious** by Will Byington, courtesy Sixthman. **Mark Henry** courtesy WWE & Ricky Media. **Bruno Sammartino** from co-author's collection. **Salina de la Renta** by Harry Aaron, courtesy MLW. **Chris Jericho** by Will Byington, courtesy Sixthman. **All others by Ed Battes, settaBPhoto.com.**

Library of Congress Cataloging-in-Publication Data

Ferris, D.X. • Paltrowitz, Darren.
Good Advice From Professional Wrestling.
Includes bibliographical references.
ISBN-13: 978-0-9975979-4-3 (pbk..: alk. Paper)
ISBN-10: 0-9975979-4-1
1. Leadership 2. Professional Wrestling 3. Success—Psychological Aspects 4. Interpersonal Relations I. Title

19062531R00093